First World War
and Army of Occupation
War Diary
France, Belgium and Germany

37 DIVISION
112 Infantry Brigade
Loyal North Lancashire Regiment
10th Battalion
30 July 1915 - 21 February 1918

WO95/2538/1

The Naval & Military Press Ltd
www.nmarchive.com
Published in association with The National Archives

Published by

The Naval & Military Press Ltd

Unit 10 Ridgewood Industrial Park,

Uckfield, East Sussex,

TN22 5QE England

Tel: +44 (0) 1825 749494

www.naval-military-press.com

www.nmarchive.com

This diary has been reprinted in facsimile from the original. Any imperfections are inevitably reproduced and the quality may fall short of modern type and cartographic standards.

© **Crown Copyright**
Images reproduced by permission of The National Archives, London, England, 2015.

Contents

Document type	Place/Title	Date From	Date To
Heading	WO95/2538/1		
Heading	37th Division 112th Infy Bde 10th Bn Loy. Nth Lancs Regt. Aug 1915-Feb 1918		
Heading	112th Inf. Bde. 37th Div. Battn. Disembarked Boulogne From England 1.8.15. 10th Battn. The Loyal North Lancashire Regiment. August (30.7.15 to 31.8.15) 1915		
Heading	War Diary Of 10th (S) Bn Loyal North Lancashire Rgt. From July 30.1915. To August 31.1915. (Volume 1)		
War Diary	Andover (Windmill Hill)	30/07/1915	31/07/1915
War Diary	Boulogne	01/08/1915	02/08/1915
War Diary	Nordausques	03/08/1915	04/08/1915
War Diary	Arques	05/08/1915	05/08/1915
War Diary	Hazebrouck	06/08/1915	20/08/1915
War Diary	L'Hoffand	21/08/1915	24/08/1915
War Diary	Godewaersvelde	25/08/1915	26/08/1915
War Diary	Orville	27/08/1915	27/08/1915
War Diary	Englebelmer	28/08/1915	31/08/1915
Heading	112th Inf, Bde. 37th Div. 10th Battn. The Loyal North Lancashire Regiment. September 1915		
Heading	War Diary Of 10th (S) Bn Loyal North Lancashire Regt. From Sept 1.1915 To Sept. 30 (Volume II)		
War Diary	Englebelmer	01/09/1915	05/09/1915
War Diary	St Amand	06/09/1915	15/09/1915
War Diary	Hannes Camps	19/09/1915	21/09/1915
War Diary	Bienvillers	22/09/1915	27/09/1915
War Diary	La Cauchie	27/09/1915	30/09/1915
Miscellaneous	Appendix A.		
Miscellaneous	Appendix 1.		
Miscellaneous	Points To Which Attention Should Be Directed During Tours Of Instruction In Trenches		
Miscellaneous Map	Plan No. 1.		
Heading	10th Battn. The Loyal North Lancashire Regiment. October 1915		
Heading	War Diary Of 10th (S) Bn Loyal N. Lancashire Regt. From 1.10.15 To 31.10.15 (Volume III)		
War Diary	La Cauchie	01/10/1915	07/10/1915
War Diary	Hannes Camps	09/10/1915	15/10/1915
War Diary	Bienvillers	16/10/1915	21/10/1915
War Diary	Humbercamps	21/10/1915	31/10/1915
Heading	10th Battn. The Loyal North Lancashire Regiment. November 1915		
Heading	War Diary Of The 10th S. Bn Loyal N. Lancs. Rgt. Part IV Nov. 1 To Nov. 30 1915		
War Diary	Humbercamps	01/11/1915	01/11/1915
War Diary	Hannescamps	02/11/1915	08/11/1915
War Diary	Bienvillers	09/11/1915	14/11/1915
War Diary	Humbercamp	14/11/1915	26/11/1915
War Diary	Hannescamp	26/11/1915	29/11/1915

Heading	10th Battn. The Loyal North Lancashire Regiment. December 1915		
Heading	War Diary 10th S. Bn Loyal N. Lancs Rgt. Dec 1.1915-Dec 31.1915 Part. V.		
War Diary	Bienvillers	01/12/1915	02/12/1915
War Diary	Hannes Camps	03/12/1915	05/12/1915
War Diary	Bienvillers	06/12/1915	08/12/1915
War Diary	Humber Camps	08/12/1915	20/12/1915
War Diary	Hannes Camps	20/12/1915	26/12/1915
War Diary	Bienvillers	26/12/1915	31/12/1915
Heading	1/10th Loyal North Lancashire Regiment January 1916		
War Diary	Bienvillers	01/01/1916	01/01/1916
War Diary	Humber Camps	01/01/1916	13/01/1916
War Diary	Hannes Camps	13/01/1916	19/01/1916
War Diary	Bienvillers	19/01/1916	25/01/1916
War Diary	Humber Camps	25/01/1916	31/01/1916
Heading	1/10th Loyal North Lancashire Regiment February 1916		
War Diary	Humber Camps	01/02/1916	01/02/1916
War Diary	Hannes Camps	06/02/1916	10/02/1916
War Diary	Bienvillers	10/02/1916	13/02/1916
War Diary	Pommier	13/02/1916	16/02/1916
War Diary	Ravine	16/02/1916	22/02/1916
War Diary	Pommier	23/02/1916	28/02/1916
War Diary	Hannescamp	29/02/1916	29/02/1916
Heading	1/10th. Loyal North Lancashire Regiment March 1916		
War Diary	Hannescamp	01/03/1916	06/03/1916
War Diary	Bienvillers	07/03/1916	08/03/1916
War Diary	No. 3 Bn.	08/03/1916	12/03/1916
War Diary	Fonque-Villers	12/03/1916	18/03/1916
War Diary	Pommier	19/03/1916	19/03/1916
War Diary	Humber Camps	20/03/1916	31/03/1916
Heading	1/10th Loyal North Lancashire Regiment April 1916		
War Diary	Humber Camps	01/04/1916	08/04/1916
War Diary	Warluzel	09/04/1916	30/04/1916
Heading	1/10th Loyal North Lancashire Regiment May 1916		
War Diary	Warluzel	01/05/1916	01/05/1916
War Diary	Pommier	02/05/1916	02/05/1916
War Diary	Bienvillers	03/05/1916	08/05/1916
War Diary	Trenches	09/05/1916	14/05/1916
War Diary	Saulty	15/05/1916	26/05/1916
War Diary	Bienvillers	26/05/1916	31/05/1916
Heading	1/10th Battalion Loyal North Lancashire Regiment June 1916		
War Diary	Bienvillers	01/06/1916	01/06/1916
War Diary	Trenches	02/06/1916	06/06/1916
War Diary	Saulty	07/06/1916	18/06/1916
War Diary	Bienvillers	18/06/1916	22/06/1916
War Diary	Trenches	23/06/1916	30/06/1916
Heading	1/10th Battalion Loyal North Lancashire Regiment July 1916		
War Diary	Trenches	01/07/1916	02/07/1916
War Diary	Halloy	03/07/1916	05/07/1916
War Diary	Millencourt	06/07/1916	06/07/1916
War Diary	Albert	07/07/1916	08/07/1916
War Diary	Tara Hill	09/07/1916	10/07/1916
War Diary	Trenches	11/07/1916	19/07/1916

War Diary	Tara Hill	19/07/1916	26/07/1916
War Diary	Albert	21/07/1916	21/07/1916
War Diary	La Houssaye	22/07/1916	30/07/1916
War Diary	Bresle	31/07/1916	31/07/1916
War Diary	Becourt Wood	31/07/1916	31/07/1916
Heading	1/10th Battalion The Loyal North Lancashire Regiment August 1916		
War Diary	Becourt Wood	01/08/1916	05/08/1916
War Diary	Mametz Wood	06/08/1916	09/08/1916
War Diary	Bazentin-Le-Petit	10/08/1916	11/08/1916
War Diary	Mametz Wood	09/08/1916	09/08/1916
War Diary	Bazentin-Le-Petit	10/08/1916	13/08/1916
War Diary	Bresle	14/08/1916	14/08/1916
War Diary	La Houssaye	15/08/1916	17/08/1916
War Diary	Longpre	18/08/1916	20/08/1916
War Diary	Noeuf Berquin	20/08/1916	22/08/1916
War Diary	Bruay	23/08/1916	24/08/1916
War Diary	Mazingarbe	24/08/1916	28/08/1916
War Diary	Trenches	29/08/1916	31/08/1916
War Diary	Mazingarbe	01/09/1916	01/09/1916
Heading	10th Loyal North Lancs August Report On Operations 11th August 1916		
Miscellaneous	B.G.C 112th Brigade 5-25 am 13 Aug.	13/08/1916	13/08/1916
Miscellaneous	B.G.C 112th Brigade 6.30 am Aug 11th	11/08/1916	11/08/1916
Miscellaneous	B.G.C 112th Brigade	11/08/1916	11/08/1916
Miscellaneous	B.G.C 112th Brigade 6.30 am Aug 11th	11/08/1916	11/08/1916
Heading	1/10th Battalion Loyal North Lancashire Regiment September 1916		
War Diary	Mazingarbe	01/09/1916	01/09/1916
War Diary	Beugin	02/09/1916	17/09/1916
War Diary	Hersin	18/09/1916	18/09/1916
War Diary	Fosse 10	19/09/1916	24/09/1916
War Diary	Trenches	25/09/1916	30/09/1916
Heading	1/10th Loyal North Lancashire Regiment October 1916		
War Diary	Bally Grenay	01/10/1916	06/10/1916
War Diary	Trenches	07/10/1916	12/10/1916
War Diary	Fosse 10	13/10/1916	14/10/1916
War Diary	Hermin	15/10/1916	15/10/1916
War Diary	Dieval	16/10/1916	17/10/1916
War Diary	Averdoingt	18/10/1916	19/10/1916
War Diary	Sericourt	20/10/1916	20/10/1916
War Diary	Hem	21/10/1916	21/10/1916
War Diary	Marieux	22/10/1916	22/10/1916
War Diary	Beausart	23/10/1916	24/10/1916
War Diary	Vauchelles	25/10/1916	29/10/1916
War Diary	Amplier	30/10/1916	30/10/1916
War Diary	Doullens	31/10/1916	31/10/1916
Heading	1/10th Loyal North Lancashire Regiment November 1916		
War Diary	Doullens	01/11/1916	11/11/1916
War Diary	Vauchelles	12/11/1916	12/11/1916
War Diary	Bertrancourt	13/11/1916	13/11/1916
War Diary	Mailly Maillet	14/11/1916	15/11/1916
War Diary	Original German 3rd Line Trenches	15/11/1916	16/11/1916
War Diary	Mailley Maillet	17/11/1916	17/11/1916
War Diary	Englebelmer	17/11/1916	17/11/1916

War Diary	Station Rd Between Beaumont-Hamel And Beaucourt	18/11/1916	22/11/1916
War Diary	Trenches	23/11/1916	23/11/1916
War Diary	Original 1st Line German Trenches	24/11/1916	24/11/1916
War Diary	Englebelmer	24/11/1916	25/11/1916
War Diary	Mailly-Maillet	26/11/1916	26/11/1916
War Diary	Acheux Wood	27/11/1916	29/11/1916
War Diary	Rubempre	30/11/1916	30/11/1916
Miscellaneous	Report Re-Fifth Army SG 72/94	22/11/1916	22/11/1916
Miscellaneous	37th Division No. G. 1086	24/11/1916	24/11/1916
Miscellaneous	Fifth Army SG 72/94	22/11/1916	22/11/1916
Miscellaneous	B.G.C., 112th Brigade.	23/11/1916	23/11/1916
Heading	1/10th Loyal North Lancashire Regiment December 1916		
War Diary	Rubempre	01/12/1916	12/12/1916
War Diary	Beauval	13/12/1916	13/12/1916
War Diary	Bonnieres	14/12/1916	14/12/1916
War Diary	Ecoivres Framecourt	15/12/1916	15/12/1916
War Diary	Bours	16/12/1916	16/12/1916
War Diary	Hurionville	17/12/1916	17/12/1916
War Diary	Carvin (Rolicque)	18/12/1916	19/12/1916
War Diary	Le Touret	20/12/1916	21/12/1916
War Diary	Haystack Post (Trenches)	22/12/1916	22/12/1916
War Diary	Trenches	23/12/1916	28/12/1916
War Diary	Le Touret	29/12/1916	31/12/1916
Heading	War Diary Of The 10th (S) Bn Loyal North Lancs January 1st 1917 To January 31st 1917 Vol No. XVIII		
War Diary	Le Touret	01/01/1917	02/01/1917
War Diary	Trenches	03/01/1917	08/01/1917
War Diary	Le Touret	09/01/1917	14/01/1917
War Diary	Trenches	15/01/1917	21/01/1917
War Diary	Le Touret	21/01/1917	27/01/1917
War Diary	La Cix Marmuse	28/01/1917	31/01/1917
Heading	War Diary Of The 10th (S) Bn The Loyal North Lancs Feb 1st 1917 To Feb 28 1917 Vol No. XIX		
War Diary	La Croix Marmuse	01/02/1917	09/02/1917
War Diary	Les Brebis	10/02/1917	10/02/1917
War Diary	Loos (Halchetts)	11/02/1917	12/02/1917
War Diary	Loos Trenches	12/02/1917	16/02/1917
War Diary	Maroc	17/02/1917	22/02/1917
War Diary	Loos	23/02/1917	23/02/1917
War Diary	Trenches	24/02/1917	26/02/1917
War Diary	Les Brebis	27/02/1917	28/02/1917
Miscellaneous	112th Bde	31/03/1917	31/03/1917
War Diary	Les Brebis	01/03/1917	01/03/1917
War Diary	Bethune	02/03/1917	02/03/1917
War Diary	Robeeq	03/03/1917	04/03/1917
War Diary	St Hilaire	05/03/1917	05/03/1917
War Diary	Laires	06/03/1917	07/03/1917
War Diary	Tangry	08/03/1917	08/03/1917
War Diary	Etree-Wamin	09/03/1917	31/03/1917
Heading	War Diary For April 1917 10th Loyal North Lancashire Regt Vol 21		
War Diary	Etree Wamin	01/04/1917	06/04/1917
War Diary	Habarcq	07/04/1917	08/04/1917
War Diary	Warlus	08/04/1917	08/04/1917
War Diary	Arras	09/04/1917	11/04/1917

War Diary	Tilloy Wood	12/04/1917	12/04/1917
War Diary	Arras	13/04/1917	13/04/1917
War Diary	Wanquetin	14/04/1917	14/04/1917
War Diary	Ambrines	14/04/1917	19/04/1917
War Diary	Habarcq	20/04/1917	20/04/1917
War Diary	Habarch	21/04/1917	21/04/1917
War Diary	St Nicholas	22/04/1917	29/04/1917
War Diary	Ambrines	29/04/1917	30/04/1917
Map			
War Diary	Ambrines	01/05/1917	18/05/1917
War Diary	Montens Court	19/05/1917	19/05/1917
War Diary	Tilloy	20/05/1917	20/05/1917
War Diary	Wancourt Line	21/05/1917	21/05/1917
War Diary	Guemappe	24/05/1917	31/05/1917
Heading	War Diary 10th L.N. Lancs June 1917 Vol 23		
Miscellaneous	To Hdqrs 112th Inf Bgde	01/07/1917	01/07/1917
War Diary	Duisans	01/06/1917	03/06/1917
War Diary	Villers-Sur-Simon	04/06/1917	07/06/1917
War Diary	Court	07/06/1917	07/06/1917
War Diary	Valhoun	08/06/1917	08/06/1917
War Diary	Capelle-Sur La-Lys	09/06/1917	22/06/1917
War Diary	Wittes	23/06/1917	23/06/1917
War Diary	Hondeghem	24/06/1917	24/06/1917
War Diary	Locre	25/06/1917	29/06/1917
War Diary	Kemmel	30/06/1917	30/06/1917
Heading	War Diary 10th L N Lancs July 1917 Vol 24		
War Diary	Kemmel	01/07/1917	01/07/1917
War Diary	Near Kemmel	02/07/1917	18/07/1917
War Diary	In The Trenches	19/07/1917	25/07/1917
War Diary	Bearer Hall	26/07/1917	26/07/1917
War Diary	Dranoutre	27/07/1917	31/07/1917
Heading	War Diary 10th L.N. Lancs Aug 1917 Vol 25		
War Diary	Dranoutre	01/08/1917	02/08/1917
War Diary	North Lancs Village	03/08/1917	06/08/1917
War Diary	Near Kemmel	07/08/1917	07/08/1917
War Diary	In The Trenches	08/08/1917	15/08/1917
War Diary	Near Kemmel	16/08/1917	21/08/1917
War Diary	In The Trenches Nr Wytchaete	22/08/1917	24/08/1917
War Diary	Near Oostaverne	25/08/1917	26/08/1917
War Diary	Near Wytchaete	27/08/1917	27/08/1917
War Diary	Irish House Nr Kemmel	28/08/1917	31/08/1917
Heading	War Diary 10th L.N. Lancs Sept 1917 Vol 26		
War Diary	Irish House	01/09/1917	02/09/1917
War Diary	In The Trenches	03/09/1917	12/09/1917
War Diary	Corunna Camp	13/09/1917	19/09/1917
War Diary	Irish House	20/09/1917	20/09/1917
War Diary	Bois Carre	21/09/1917	21/09/1917
War Diary	Corunna Camp	22/09/1917	22/09/1917
War Diary	In The Line	23/09/1917	27/09/1917
War Diary	Near Kemmel	28/09/1917	28/09/1917
War Diary	Near Vierstraat	29/09/1917	30/09/1917
Heading	War Diary Of 10th (Service) Battalion Loyal North Lancashire Regiment From 1st October 1917 To 31st October 1917 Volume 26		
War Diary	Willibeek Camp	01/10/1917	05/10/1917
War Diary	Tower Hamlets	05/10/1917	10/10/1917

War Diary	Willebeek Camp	11/10/1917	12/10/1917
War Diary	Corunna Camp	13/10/1917	15/10/1917
War Diary	Ypres	16/10/1917	22/10/1917
War Diary	Corunna Camp	23/10/1917	26/10/1917
War Diary	Birr Barracks	27/10/1917	27/10/1917
War Diary	Locre	28/10/1917	08/11/1917
War Diary	Bois Carre	09/11/1917	09/11/1917
War Diary	In The Trenches	10/11/1917	10/11/1917
War Diary	Spoil Bank	11/11/1917	13/11/1917
War Diary	In The Trenches	13/11/1917	17/11/1917
War Diary	Bois Carre	18/11/1917	25/11/1917
War Diary	La Clytte	25/11/1917	05/12/1917
War Diary	In The Trenches	06/12/1917	13/12/1917
War Diary	Ridge Wood	14/12/1917	24/12/1917
War Diary	Murrumbidgee Camp	25/12/1917	28/12/1917
War Diary	In The Trenches	29/12/1917	05/01/1918
War Diary	Ridge Wood	06/01/1918	10/01/1918
War Diary	Wallon Cappel	11/01/1918	21/01/1918
War Diary	Vierstraat	22/01/1918	04/02/1918
War Diary	Racquinghem	05/02/1918	16/02/1918
War Diary	Wippenhoek	17/02/1918	21/02/1918

wa95/2538/t

37TH DIVISION
112TH INFY BDE

10TH BN LOY.NTH LANCS REGT.
AUG 1915 - FEB 1918.

DISBANDED

112th Inf.Bde.
37th Div.

Battn. disembarked
Boulogne from
England 1.8.15.

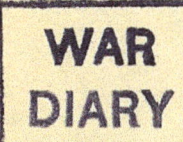

10th BATTN. THE LOYAL NORTH LANCASHIRE REGIMENT.

A U G U S T

(30.7.15 to 31.8.15)

1 9 1 5

Jan '18

CONFIDENTIAL.

WAR DIARY

OF

10TH (S.) Bn. Loyal North Lancashire Regt.

From July 20, 1915.   To August 31, 1915.

(VOLUME 1.)

Desmond Coke,
Capt. & Adjt.,
10th Loyal N. Lancs.

10th S. Bn. L. N. Lan. R.

Army Form C. 2118.

WAR DIARY
INTELLIGENCE SUMMARY
(Erase heading not required.)

Instructions regarding War Diaries and Intelligence Summaries are contained in F. S. Regs., Part II. and the Staff Manual respectively. Title pages will be prepared in manuscript.

Place	Date	Hour	Summary of Events and Information	Remarks and references to Appendices
ANDOVER	July 30/31	5 A.M.	Transport Party entrained. Officers, 3: Other Ranks, 109.	D.C.
Hundred Hill	31.15	5.50 P.M.	Battalion entrained in two trains: LUDGERSHALL Station: Officers, 28: O.R., 846.	D.C.
BOULOGNE	Aug.1	2 A.M.	Arrived at BOULOGNE. Marched to OSTROHOVE Rest Camp. Underfeaters joined.	D.C.
"	"	Aug.2 8:10 A	Proceeded by train to AUDRUICQ. Left 2 men in Hospital at BOULOGNE. Marched to NORDAUSQUES.	D.C.
NORDAUSQUES	Aug.3	—	In billets at NORDAUSQUES.	D.C.
"	Aug.4	9 A.M.	Marched to ARQUES. Arrived 4 p.m.	D.C.
ARQUES	Aug.5	7:30 A.M.	Marched to HAZEBROUCK. Left 4 men in Hospital at ARQUES. Arrived 3.12 p.m.	D.C.
HAZEBROUCK	Aug.6	—	In billets, A farme, Rue de Flerville.	D.C.
"	Aug.7	—	In billets. Strength, O.29: O.R. 946.	D.C.
"	Aug.8	—	In billets.	D.C.
"	Aug.9	—	In billets. Chaplain (Capt. A Gossen) left, on transfer to 1st Division.	D.C.
"	Aug.10	6 A.M.	In billets. A working party of 569 men left for LOCRE under Major A McC. WEBSTER	D.C.
"	Aug.11	—	In billets. 2nd Lt H.S. Roxen sent to hospital, having injured knee (not on duty.)	D.C.
"	Aug.12	—	In billets.	D.C.
"	Aug.13	—	In billets.	D.C.
"	Aug.14	—	In billets. Strength, O.28: O.R. 942.	D.C.
"	Aug.15	—	In billets.	D.C.

Army Form C. 2118

WAR DIARY

~~INTELLIGENCE SUMMARY~~

(Erase heading not required.)

Instructions regarding War Diaries and Intelligence Summaries are contained in F.S. Regs., Part II. and the Staff Manual respectively. Title Pages will be prepared in manuscript.

Place	Date	Hour	Summary of Events and Information	Remarks and references to Appendices
HAZEBROUCK	Aug 16	—	In billets.	A.C.
"	Aug 17	—	In billets.	A.C.
"	Aug 18	—	In billets.	A.C.
"	Aug 19	—	In billets.	A.C.
"	Aug 20	10 A.M.	HAZEBROUCK. Battn. moved, under Divl. Orders, to new billets on BORRÉ Road	A.C.
L'HOFFAND	Aug 21	—	L'HOFFAND. Marching-out state: Officers, 11; O.R. 364. Sick: Officer, 1; O.R., 10; On command: Officers, 2; Other Ranks, 6.	P.C.
"	Aug 22	—	In billets.	A.C.
"	Aug 23	—	In billets. Strength of Bn. O. 28; O.R., 932.	A.C.
"	Aug 24	1.45 PM	HAZEBROUCK Battn (6) moved by road to GODEWAERSVELDE, where it united with the LOCRE party & went into billets for the night.	D.C.
GODEWAER-SVELDE	Aug 25	—	In billets.	D.C.
GODEWAER-SVELDE	Aug 26	0-13	Battalion entrained & proceeded by rail to DOULLENS, whence it marched to ORVILLE, arriving 10.15 A.M. & went into billets. Lieut-Genl Sir Thomas Snow, VIII Army Corps Commander, addressed the officers of the Bn. at 2.30 p.m., on the transfer of the 37th Divn. to the VII Army Corps.	D.C.
ORVILLE.	Aug 27	9.0	Marched to ENGLEBELMER, on being attached to the 11th Infy. Bde. for instructional purposes & proceeded into billets, 16.55.	D.C.
ENGLE-BELMER.	Aug 28	—	In billets. Lectures; visits to trenches; night digging: &c. Strength O 26; O.R. 919.	D.C.
"	Aug 29	20.30	"A" Coy under Capt. C.R. MAUDE, (6 Officers; 208 O.R.) went into 1st Hants Trenches for 3 nights' instruction. "C" Coy under Capt. H.F. KING (6 Offs; 194 O.R.) into 1st Rifle Bde.	D.C.
"	Aug 30	—	Instruction & digging carried on by Remainder of Battalion. 1 man wounded during night digging.	D.C.
"	Aug 31	—	Ditto ditto. Practice in bomb throwing, &c. Night digging. 1 man (A Coy) wounded in trenches.	D.C.

112th Inf. Bde.
37th Div.

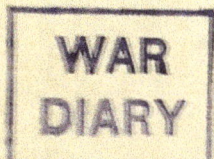

10th BATTN. THE LOYAL NORTH LANCASHIRE REGIMENT.

S E P T E M B E R

1 9 1 5

Attached:

Appendix A.
Plan No. 1.

CONFIDENTIAL.

WAR DIARY
OF
10ᵀᴴ (S.) Bⁿ Loyal North Lancashire Regt.

From Sept. 1. 1915 To Sept. 30.

(VOLUME II.)

WAR DIARY
or
INTELLIGENCE SUMMARY.
(Erase heading not required.)

Army Form C. 2118.

Place	Date	Hour	Summary of Events and Information	Remarks and references to Appendices
ENGLEBELMER	Sept.1.	20.30.	"B" Company, under Major MILVAIN, (6 O: 200, O.R.) with the C.O. (Colonel N. Dennys) at Adjutant, (Capt. Desmond Coke) at M.G. Section under 2t H.F. Williams, (O.R. 27) proceeded into 1st Hants trenches: "D" Coy, under Capt. DRYDEN, (O, 6; O.R. 205,) into the 1st Rifles, for instructional purposes.	D.C. For scheme of training which attached to XI Bde; see APPENDIX I
"	Sept 2.	—	1st Hants trenches bombarded 6.15 - 6.45 by trench mortars. 1 man, L.N. Lewis wounded. [2 men 1st Hants killed; 2nd Lt Dale & 1 man wounded.] training continued.	D.C.
"	Sept 5.	8.15.	Battalion marched, on conclusion of attachment to 11th Bde, to ST AMAND, proceeded into billets, joining up with the rest of 112th Bde as Brigade in reserve. Marching out state: Officers, 28. Other Ranks, 917.	D.C.
ST AMAND.	Sept 6.	11.50.	Draft of 60 Other Ranks arrived from 11th Battalion.	D.C.
" "	Sept 15.	19.30.	Battalion relieved 13th King's Royal Rifles in the trenches. Marching-out state, O, 27; Quartermaster & Transport Officer remained in billets at ST AMAND with their respective departments): O.R. 934. All 4 Companies went into the firing line, which is shown on an attached rough Plan,) & were disposed as follows: "B Coy, trench 56-58 inclusive; "A" Coy, 59-61; "C" Coy, 62-65; "D" Coy, 66-68: the right Company (B) entering via FONCQUEVILLERS, the other three via HANNESCAMPS. The relief was completed about 1.15 A.M., 16th.	D.C. See Plan No 1.

Army Form C. 2118

WAR DIARY
or
INTELLIGENCE SUMMARY
(Erase heading not required.)

Instructions regarding War Diaries and Intelligence Summaries are contained in F.S. Regs., Part II. and the Staff Manual respectively. Title Pages will be prepared in manuscript.

Place	Date	Hour	Summary of Events and Information	Remarks and references to Appendices
HANNESCAMPS.	16/9.	—	Work begun on all portions of the sector. The French, who had occupied the trenches till about 12 days previous, (when the 111th Bde took them over,) were found to have left excellent dug-outs & elaborate communication trenches: but the parapets were thin, sometimes with dug-outs undermining them, & there was a great scarcity of traverses. Many exposed portions of the trench also called for deepening. The general impression conveyed was that this part of the line, — owing partly, perhaps, to there being almost 1000 yds. between the opposing forces, — had been considered so safe that comfort was reckoned more important than considerations of Defence.	A.C.
"	17–20.		These days were quiet. The enemy but a certain number of small shells into the trenches, & rather more on to points around B" H.Q. at HANNESCAMPS; but no real damage was done nor were there any casualties. The enemy shewed heavy fire daily, with rifle & machine-gun, at both morning & evening stand-to, & snipers were extremely active during the first part of this period. Steps were taken to improve our wire, which was found to be thin at places. A patrol under 2nd Lt. E. Howell reached the enemy wire & reported it to be extremely thick & with long barbs. They also reported that the German line must be very thinly held at night, anyhow in the fire-trenches, at this point, as no sound could be heard of any movement, & no action was taken. Enemy patrols, however, were observed & an elaborate German work, supposedly a pumping-station, was located at C.11.b.5.5. (Ref. Claw Directory 20,000.) 6th (London) 185 Bde R.F.A. was informed & shelled it with shrapnel on the 20th. The result was unknown, but not to destroy the work. The actual pump was, however,	

Army Form C. 2118

WAR DIARY
or
INTELLIGENCE SUMMARY
(Erase heading not required)

Instructions regarding War Diaries and Intelligence Summaries are contained in F.S. Regs., Part II. and the Staff Manual respectively. Title Pages will be prepared in manuscript.

Place	Date	Hour	Summary of Events and Information	Remarks and references to Appendices
HANNESCAMPS.	21/9 —	—	remained during the night 20/21. During this same night our wires were cut, under orders from the 112th Bde., an opening being made opposite the front of each Platoon. This was effected without casualties. At 4.15 P.M, Lieut. H.P. Williams, M.G.O., was wounded by shrapnel & was sent to the Base. O.R., 1 slightly; at duty. At 1.15 A.M. whilst 2nd Lieut. C.A.S. Bidwell was returning from a listening post through his newly-cut wire-opening, four Germans suddenly leapt up close to him. He challenged & they fired point blank. 2nd Lt. Bidwell was killed instantly. Wounded 1 O.R. (since dead.) At 7 A.M., 3 enemy shells landed on trench 63. Wounded, 2 O.R. (1 since dead.) At 6 P.M. the first Platoon of the 6th Bedfordshire Regt, 112th Inf. Bde, relieving, passed Bn. Hd. Qrs., & at 8.20 P.M. the relief was reported complete. The Battalion went into billets at BIENVILLERS as Battalion in Reserve. At 11.30 P.M. digging parties were sent out.	D.C.
BIENVILLERS.	22/9 —25/	—	Digging parties found daily :— 150 men at 8 A.M. + again 7.30 P.M. 150 " " 12.30 P.M. " " 11.30 P.M. 50 " " 8.30 A.M. " " 8 P.M. 50 " " 1 P.M. " " 12 M.N. 3 each shift working for 4 hrs. A company was also detailed as Infantry Piequet. 2 Platoons of which proceeded nightly to the support trenches between CHISWICK AVENUE & the HAN-NESCAMPS — LES ESSARTS road, in support of the Centre Battⁿ, worked in 2 4-hr. shifts. Capt. G.W. Ainsworth left for PAS, to go through a course of Administrative Staff work, on the 24th. Strength, 27.9.15 : Officers, 27 ; Other Ranks, 972.	A.C.
LA CAUCHIE.	27.	—	Battⁿ. The Battalion was relieved by 13th K.R.R. Relief completed, 9.5. P.M. The Battⁿ. proceeded into billets at LA CAUCHIE; the remainder of the 112th Bde in	D.C.

Army Form C. 2118

WAR DIARY
or
INTELLIGENCE SUMMARY
(Erase heading not required.)

Instructions regarding War Diaries and Intelligence Summaries are contained in F.S. Regs., Part II. and the Staff Manual respectively. Title Pages will be prepared in manuscript.

Place	Date	Hour	Summary of Events and Information	Remarks and references to Appendices
LA CAUCHIE	28-30.		Reserve.) Proceeding into billets at HUMBERCAMP. In billets. Route marches, digging on VII Corps line, etc.	D.C.

G Desmond Coke
Capt. & Adjt. 10 L.N. Lancs. Regt.
2-10.15.

A P P E N D I X   A.

APPENDIX I.

Appendix "A"

Programme of Work.

A & C. Coys complete   B & D Coys complete

Date.	Bn. Hd. Qrs.	2 Coys (A & C)	2 Coys (B & D)	M.G. Section.
Aug. 29th.	Q.Mr. and Trans. Offr. will be attached to the Transport of some L.I. now at ENGLEBELMER.	9.0 am. Lecture on entrenchments and see ENGLEBELMER entrenchment. 10.0 am. Lecture on French duties. 2-4 pm. Digging. 2.0 pm. 1. Offr. per Coy. to be at Bde. H.Q. where guides will meet them and take them to Bn. H.Q. so that they can arrange for going into trenches 29th.	9 am. Lecture on entrenchment. 10.30 and 12.30 am. } Digging. 2 pm. Lecture on French duties. 7 pm. Offr. at Bde. H.Q. MARTINSART when Bns. will show them second line and work proposed.	Offr. and N.C.O. will go round with Bde. Bde. Offr. Reconnoitre N.E. east of VITERMONT. Will return about 2 pm. Left Sector.
29th.	Offr. and Regt. Mann. 9-11. am. through files regarding various local orders etc. 2. Offrs. per H.Q. to be attached to H.Q. Staff Bn.: C. Coy at 8 pm.	9-11. am. Revetting and mining. 12 noon Lecture on interior economy. One Coy. to be at N.E. corner BOIS d'AVELUY. at 8.30 pm and then move to trenches Right Sector with Hants. One coy to be at 8.30 pm at H.Q. Centre Sector at 8.30 pm and go into R.F of Bde. trenches.	9 am. Lecture on Interior economy in trenches. 10-12 pm. Revetting and wiring. 8.30 pm. Two Coys to be at MESNIL STN where guide will take them to entrenching ground. Digging up to 1 a.m. 100% shovels 100% picks	9 am. Lecture by Bde. M.G. Offr.
30th.	Trenches.		11 am. Offrs and Section Commdrs. to see MESNIL Defences. Offr. Comdg. will provide guides to meet them at Southern Entrance. 8.30 pm. Digging as for 29th.	Offr. and N.C.O's will go round Right Sector with Bde. M.G. Offr. Rendezvous Bde. H.Q. MARTINSART at 10 a.m.

(CONTD).

Date	B & H Coy	A Coy.	B Coy.	M.G. Section
		Trenches.		
	Off. and half to be attached to trenches to be out at 9 pm	Out - anything after 9 pm.	1 Off. & 60 Coy arr'd N.C.O. & 15 station to be at Polka Hill at 9 am, rations carried, will take Bevan to Kn M and they will arrange for carrying into trenches. 9.30 pm. To dig in trs at Polk and J Dig see bar. One coy to be at N.E. corner of Bois L'AVEQUE at 9.30 pm, one coy into trench, others one coy to be at K. Conter before and more into R.E. Reg. trenches	Officers to arrange for men in 2 or 3 afternoon relief to make arrangements (Reg Coy &c)
		Rapid digging. To be at MESNIL EAN at 9.30 pm, carrying 50 picks	Trenches	Trenches
		1 Coy. Off. and 50 Coy Sgt. founded to be at MESNIL SEVERAL will assist our men at sentry entrance to trenches of village, the one will be ready by 4 am the other digging at far end at 9.30 pm.	Trenches	Trenches
		Digging as for 2nd inst	Out - anything after 9 pm.	Out - after 9 pm.
	Instructional Post of enough done [Cancelled]			

POINTS TO WHICH ATTENTION SHOULD BE DIRECTED DURING TOURS OF INSTRUCTION IN TRENCHES.

Fire trenches - dimensions, advantages and disadvantages.

Breastworks.

Supporting trenches - suitable positions for and profile for.

Field of fire - foreground.

Communication trenches - depth and direction of.

Thickness of parapet.

Height of parapet.

Revetments, sandbags, hurdles, wooden frames, etc.

Traverses - dimensions and how made.

Loophole, steel - (a) for firing through, (b) for observation.

Best positions for machine guns.

Sandbags - uses for.

Attitude and habits of the enemy should be studied.

Distribution of a company in the trenches.

Look-out system and reliefs for.

Action in case of attack.

Position of company H.Q. and intercommunication between platoons.

Telephones - speaking tubes.

Listening posts.

Spare ammunition reserve, where kept in Company trenches.

Reserve of bombs and hand grenades, periscopes, etc.

One company relieving another in the trenches.

Flooring of trenches.

Construction of dug-outs - (a) in fire trench, (b) in breastworks.

Bridges over small streams with traverses to cover gap.

Wire entanglements - where placed and various natures of.

Loose wire trips and "Chevaux de Frise".

"Very" pistols and periscopes - uses for.

Latrines in the trenches.

System of delivery of rations to units and transport of same to the trenches.

Issue of R.E. material to units - how organized and how disposed of by units.

Use of pumps in flooded trenches and system of damming portions that have become water-logged.

P L A N N O. 1.

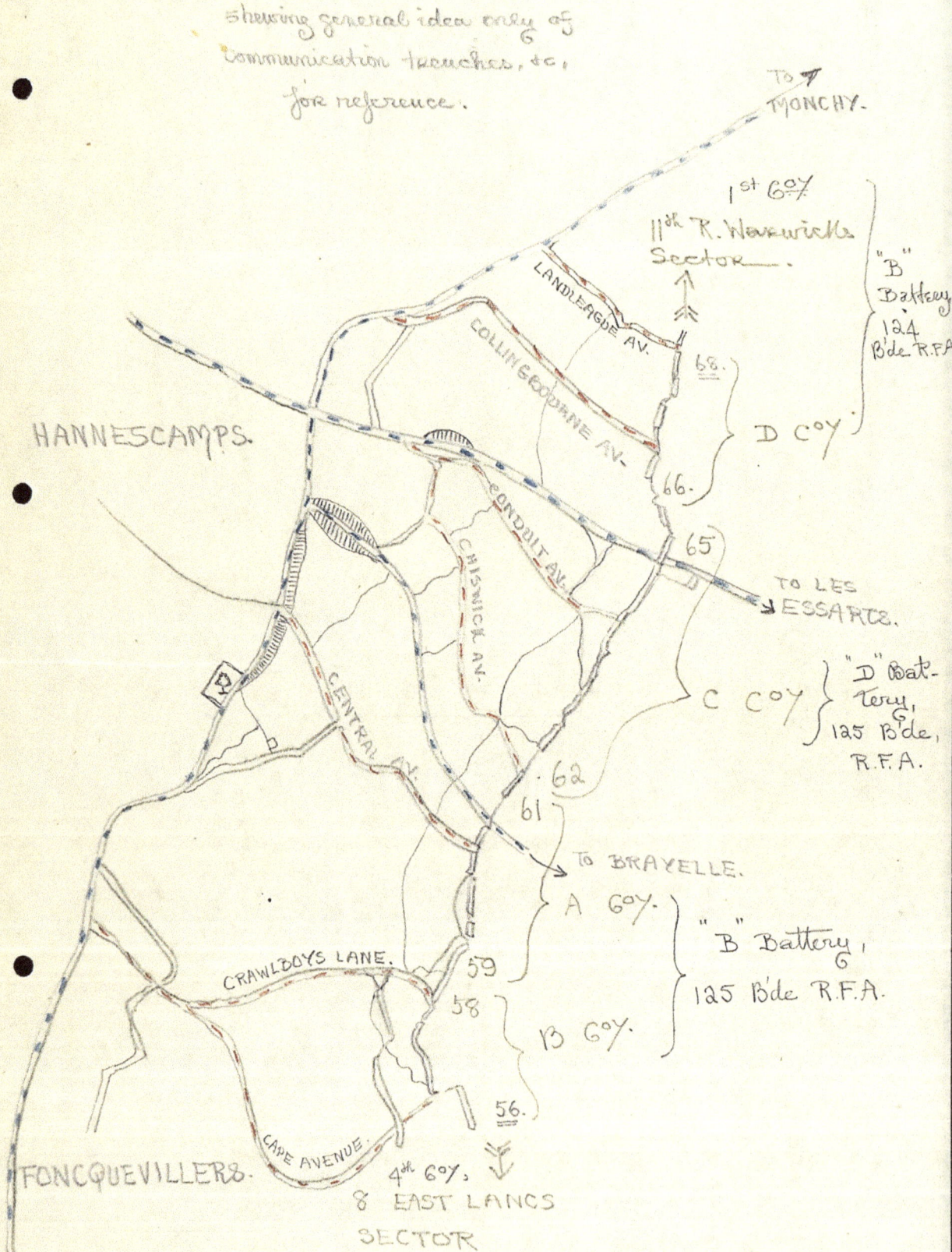

112th Inf.Bde.
37th Div.

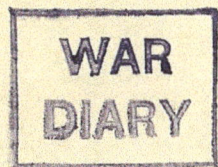

10th BATTN. THE LOYAL NORTH LANCASHIRE REGIMENT.

O C T O B E R

1 9 1 5

CONFIDENTIAL.

WAR DIARY

of

10th (S.) Bn LOYAL N. LANCASHIRE REGT.

FROM 1.10.15   TO   31.10.15.

(VOLUME III.)

WAR DIARY
INTELLIGENCE SUMMARY

Army Form C. 2118

(Erase heading not required.)

Place	Date	Hour	Summary of Events and Information	Remarks and references to Appendices
LA CAUCHIE	1.10.15	—	In billets. Digging continued on VII Corps line (600 men:) Route Marches, &c.	D.C.
"	7.10.15	—	Work begun on the defences of LA CAUCHIE; under orders from Lt. General Sir Thomas Snow in person.	D.C.
ANNESCAMPS	9.10.15	6 P.M.	The Battalion relieved the 13th Bn. K.R.R. Rifles, the first platoon entering at 6 P.M. & the relief being completed by 7.35 P.M. The relief was effected without casualties & the night passed quietly except that snipers were found to be more active than during the last period in trenches: especially in No 4 Coy sector, (T.66-8.)	D.C.
"	10.10.15	—	At daybreak it was discovered that the Germans were working on a new line of trenches in front of the OUVRAGES BLANCS, about E.18.A.2.3. (Ref:- 57 D N.E. Sheets 1 & 2 (Parts of) 1/10,000 : Sept. 1915.)) A good view could be obtained from T.67 under cover from heavy machine-gun covering fire, that made observation from T.66 unsafe. At least 12 men could be seen burning up brown earth in front of the wire. 5 rounds rapid discouraged them, but not for long. They were believed to be joining up their line, as shown by the dotted lines below:—	D.C.

ROAD. ━ ━ ━

WIRE. 〜〜〜

0 100 200 300 400 500 YDS.

TO MONCHY

TO DOUCHY

TO HANNESCAMPS

N ↑

Army Form C. 2118

WAR DIARY
INTELLIGENCE SUMMARY
(Erase heading not required.)

Place	Date	Hour	Summary of Events and Information	Remarks and references to Appendices
HANNESCAMPS.	11./10./15.		Activity of snipers again observed, especially along the sector occupied by No 3 ("G") Coy, where one man was killed + two wounded at short intervals. The German working party in front of the OUVRAGES BLANCS was again busy at day break, but dispersed upon rapid fire being opened on them. On the 10th inst. the following order was received from 11d Qrs, 112 Inf. Bde: "With reference to the report of a patrol of the 13 K.R.R. which refers to a German trench at about 17 B.3.2., the Brigadier would like Colonel Dennys to take action against it. He suggests that perhaps an observation patrol should be sent out to-night to confirm the statement + to locate the trench, + that to-morrow night a strong patrol should be sent out to attack it." (sgd) E.Saunton, Major. This patrol on the 10th inst. having had no opportunity of good observation would owing to having encountered a stronger enemy patrol, another attempt was made during the night 11/12 to investigate the alleged new trench, strongly held by Germans, along the ESSARTS Road. Four patrols, each of 1 N.C.O. + 3 men, the whole under the command of Lieut. A. PROCTOR, were sent out from Trenches 64 + 65 at 4.30 P.M. 11.X.14 proceeded to reconnoitre the ground thoroughly. Lieut. PROCTOR took his party some 800 yards along the ESSARTS Road, but found only a disused line of trenches of which the existence was already known. This he faced out at 250 yds from the Northern listening-post of Trench 65: running both sides of the road, approximately N.E. by S.W.: parapet facing British lines: tumble-down shelters at about 8 yds interval. The new line of German trenches, pushed forward to	N.C.

WAR DIARY
INTELLIGENCE SUMMARY
(Erase heading not required.)

Army Form C. 2118

Instructions regarding War Diaries and Intelligence Summaries are contained in F.S. Regs., Part II. and the Staff Manual respectively. Title Pages will be prepared in manuscript.

Place	Date	Hour	Summary of Events and Information	Remarks and references to Appendices
ANNESCAMPS	12·10·15		when a short distance of our line, + strongly held, was thus proved to be non-existent. The patrols all returned without casualties.	

Casualties, 11.10.15 : Killed, Officers, 0 : O.R., 1 : Wounded, Officers, 0 : O.R., 2.

Capt. HEYES, B Battery, 154th Bde R.F.A., made observations from Bay 3, Trench 67, of the brown earth at about E.18.A.2.3. Four shells were fired, the first three landing slightly beyond the point, but the fourth in the actual new works. The enemy at once retaliated with two shells, which fell wide.

At about 3.35 P.M. a flight of twelve French aeroplanes, coming from the South + passing over the German lines, drew sufficient fire to prove that the enemy trenches held more men than had been at times supposed.

D.G.

At 6.25 P.M. the enemy opposite No 1 Company sector opened with heavy shrapnel + shell fire for about 10 minutes. At 6.35 P.M. four lights went up from about 2000 yds in rear of the German lines + instantly heavy machine-gun + rifle opened on trenches 56-58 + the Battalion on our right flank (8th E. Lancs). This lasted for 25 minutes + was followed by shell-fire, to which "D" Battery, 125 Bde R.F.A, retaliated. Only two men were wounded: both very slightly : + one of them was out on patrol at the time. Many of the German shells failed to explode + their artillery fire was found to be directed less on the fire-trench than on the support-trenches.

Casualties, 12.10.13 : Killed, Nil. Wounded: Officers, Nil : O.R., 3.

WAR DIARY or INTELLIGENCE SUMMARY

Army Form C. 2118

(Erase heading not required.)

Place	Date	Hour	Summary of Events and Information	Remarks and references to Appendices
HANNESCAMPS	13/10/15		An unusually quiet day & night. Patrols which went out at 4 A.M. & lay in the long grass, with the idea of sniping snipers, returned at 7 P.M. having seen no enemy snipers or patrols. Casualties: Nil.	D.C.
HANNESCAMPS	14/10/15		Another quiet day. Enemy still working. E.18.A.2.3. Machine-gun fire was opened on the party at about 4 P.M. "6" Battery, 124 Bde R.F.A., obtained 4 direct hits upon it. Another working party was sighted, 3.15 P.M, at E.23.D.6.5., & a German work brought down with rifle-fire. O.C. "B" Battery, 125 Bde R.F.A., was informed of the work in progress, but replied that his week's supply of ammunition was expended. Casualties: Nil.	D.C.
HANNESCAMPS	15/10/15		A heavy mist prevented activity of snipers & allowed Lieut. J. GRANETT, who went out with a patrol at 4 A.M., to make a proper survey of the disused German trenches. The existence of shelters was confirmed. The trench was found to be some 290 yards along the ESSARTS road from trench 65. There are three trenches South of the road, — 40, 100, & 150 yds in length, — & one North, — about 400 yds. 200 yards along the road from T.65, six kits were found & more recent work. A German paper, dated 26.9.15; a clip of German cartridges; a handkerchief with coloured map of France & the German frontier, inscribed in print, "KARTE VOM DEUTSCH-FRAZÖSISCHEN KRIEGSCHAUPLATZ, 1914," proved snipers to have used show lately. The Battalion was relieved by the 6th Bedfordshire Regt. Night 15/16. 5.30 P.M. & completed 7.45 P.M.	D.C. See rough plan (next page).

1875. Wt. W593/826 1,000,000 4/15 J.B.C. & A. A.D.S.S./Forms/C.2118.

Army Form C. 2118

WAR DIARY
~~INTELLIGENCE SUMMARY~~
(Erase heading not required.)

Instructions regarding War Diaries and Intelligence Summaries are contained in F. S. Regs, Part II. and the Staff Manual respectively. Title Pages will be prepared in manuscript.

Place	Date	Hour	Summary of Events and Information	Remarks and references to Appendices
				A.C.

ROUGH PLAN SHOWING RESULT OF THE SURVEY MADE, 15.10.15, BY LIEUT. J. GRAVETT, 10 L.N.L.

A = Sniper's post.
B = " " posts.
C = Disused German trench.

― British line.
― German line.
═ Road.

HANNES-
CAMPS.

ESSARTS ROAD

SCALE :―
0 100 200 300 400 500 YDS.

1875 Wt. W593/826 1,000,000 4/15 J.B.C. & A. A.D.S.S./Forms/C. 2118.

WAR DIARY

INTELLIGENCE SUMMARY

(Erase heading not required.)

Army Form C. 2118

Place	Date	Hour	Summary of Events and Information	Remarks and references to Appendices
ENNILLERS	16/10/15 to 20/10/15	—	Battalion in reserve to the Brigade. Digging was carried on — day & night shifts; & under Brigade Orders alarms were practised almost daily, with an unlying Company on one out working, with a view to testing the time required to occupy the sector of the subsidiary Trench line allotted to the Battalion. This was found to average out at about 35 minutes from the alarm to completion of occupation.	D.C.
HUMBERCAMPS	21/10/15 to 31/10/15	—	The Battalion was relieved by 13th King's Royal Rifles at 4 P.M. & proceeded into billets at HUMBERCAMPS. (112th Bde in Reserve.) Digging was carried on: Corps Siue, &c., by day & night. "A" Coy detached for wood-cutting at PAS. Strength, 30.10.15: Officers, 26: O.R., 970. Admitted to Hospital: (excluding wounded.) 19. Oct. Reinforcements: 14: (Draft, 9: 5 from Hospital.) 21.10.15. Officers joined: Nil.	D.C.

Desmond Coke,
Capt. & Adjt.,
10 R.S.N. Sauco. Regt.

B.E.F,
31.10.15.

112th Inf.Bde.
37th Div.

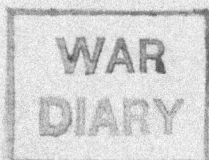

10th BATTN. THE LOYAL NORTH LANCASHIRE REGIMENT.

N O V E M B E R

1 9 1 5

CONFIDENTIAL.

WAR DIARY

OF

THE 10TH S. BN LOYAL N. LANCS. REGT.

PART IV

NOV. 1 — to — NOV. 30,

1915.

Army Form C. 2118

WAR DIARY
or
INTELLIGENCE SUMMARY
(Erase heading not required.)

Place	Date	Hour	Summary of Events and Information	Remarks and references to Appendices
OMBERCAMPS	1.11.15.	—	In billets.	
ANNESCAMPS	2.11.15.	5.20 p.m.	The Battalion relieved the 13th King's Royal Rifles, the East Platoon entering at 5.20 P.M., & the relief being complete by 8.5. P.M. The slowness of this operation was due to the bad state of the trenches. Heavy rain had fallen continuously for some days & the arrangements for draining the trenches proved to be inadequate. The low-lying sectors were from 1½ to 2 ft. deep in water; & the collapse of trench-sides formed a heavy mud. Fire-trenches 55, 59, + 68, suffered worst; the parapets & traverses falling-in & blocking the whole trench. Most of the work had been done by the R.E.; but it failed signally to stand the strain, partly perhaps through the 1 in 4 slope not being in every case, but chiefly (it is believed) through the sandbags not having been left sufficiently empty to allow for the expansion of the soil, which is of a clay nature. Several of the dug-outs were found to have collapsed & two men were buried in this way at different points; one being rescued after being buried 50 minutes, not severely injured. Work on drainage, &c., was at once begun. The enemy was quiet. Casualties: Killed, Nil. Wounded, Officers, Nil. O.R., Accidental, 3.	
ANNESCAMPS	3.11.15.	—	The long continuous rain ceased at dawn, & great progress was made with the work of drainage, assisted by parties from the 6th Bedfords (in Reserve) + the R.E.; who installed pumps at the worst points; but the damage by daylight proved	

WAR DIARY
or
INTELLIGENCE SUMMARY

(Erase heading not required.)

Army Form C. 2118

Place	Date	Hour	Summary of Events and Information	Remarks and references to Appendices
			to be serious. The enemy was again quiet, & a deserter who entered the 7th Leicesters lines about midnight, 3/4, reported these trenches to be in a worse condition than our own. Two snipers went out from T.66 about midday & settled at Sniper's Tree, which used to be a German sniping-pit; from which position they accounted for at any rate one German, working on the new trench at E.18. a.2.5.

A minenwerfer, seemingly installed since the Battalion last period in trenches, fired a number of shells, most of which went into the lines of the 8th. G. Davies, on our right flank, about 9 A.M.; the first two only falling a little short of our trenches, at T.56 & 58, where they did very slight damage. Approximate position of minenwerfer, E.23. c. 6.6.

A patrol of 2 N.C.O's & 35 men, under 2nd Lt. Lloyd, went out at 6 P.M. from T.60 & proceeded to some canvas screens, erected 500 yds East of T.60 by the 111th Bde, where they refixed the wires leading to the N. listening post of T.59. 2nd Lt. Lloyd then proceeded further East, pausing frequently to listen & covered by an advance guard. Nothing was heard: but suddenly, at E.23. a. 7.9. he was challenged in German; a red light went up; & fire was opened & bombs thrown by an enemy party estimated (from the volume of fire) at about 80 men. 2nd Lt. Lloyd was thrown to the ground & dazed, by a bomb, which severely wounded his sergeant in the eye. | |

WAR DIARY
or
INTELLIGENCE SUMMARY
(Erase heading not required.)

Army Form C. 2118

Place	Date	Hour	Summary of Events and Information	Remarks and references to Appendices
HANNESCAMPS	4/11/15	—	The rest of the patrol retaliated with both bombs & heavy fire, & the enemy made off. As however the Germans were in superior force, the patrol was near their lines, & the men had got somewhat scattered, 2nd Lt. LLOYD thought it best to return, which he did, assisting home a man wounded in five places with rifle-shot. The patrol arrived back 9 P.M. Two men were missing when the roll was called, & a later patrol failed to find them. Casualties: Killed: O.R. 1. Wounded: Officers, Nil: O.R. 2. Missing: O.R. 2. O.C. "B" 6"Y, having located an enemy gun at about E.23.d.44, informed the "A" Battery, 125 Bde R.F.A. This gun had fired a number of .77 shells into our right Company between 10 & 11 A.M. At the first & second shot the battery fired a little wide, but further directed by Major R. St MILVAIN, (O.C. "B" 6"Y, 10 L.N.L.) scored a direct hit with the third. The gun did not fire again. At 4.15 P.M, three snipers went out from T.67 to try to capture an enemy sniper observed the previous day at about 400 yds. from the trench, in a S.E. direction near the Osieu bed. At about E18.d.1.5. a single German was encountered. Dispositions were made to surround him & work in on him, when suddenly an enemy patrol of about 20 men appeared. The single German had been moving forward & backward in a seemingly aimless way, while	

WAR DIARY or INTELLIGENCE SUMMARY

Army Form C. 2118

(Erase heading not required.)

Place	Date	Hour	Summary of Events and Information	Remarks and references to Appendices
ANNESCAMPS	5/11/15	—	our men were stalking him, + it is supposed that he was a decoy to lead small patrols on to the larger party. In the present case, however, it was the enemy who were surprised. A bomb was thrown into the middle of them + our men opened rapid fire. They immediately scattered + took to their heels after only a few shots. No dead or wounded were left, however. The enemy was again quiet. Casualties : NIL.	D.C.
			The unusual inactivity of the enemy, combined with the sound of traction engines that heard nightly behind GOMMECOURT WOOD, suggested that an enemy relief must be in progress. A patrol, sent out from T.60. to the scene of the conflict with the enemy patrol two nights before. (E 23. d. 7.7.) met + heard noone. Three privates attached to the 178th Tunnelling Coy, R.E., were this day killed by an enemy mine explosion. Other Casualties : NIL.	D.C.
ANNESCAMPS	6/11/15		The enemy still very inactive. Two fighting patrols, sent out from T.58 + T.66, between 5 + 9 P.M., failed to see or hear anything + returned with the impression that the German line had been less strongly held since the supposed relief, Night 5/6th. At 3.45 P.M. a sound was heard opposite T.61. as of an aeroplane engine,	D.C.

WAR DIARY
or
INTELLIGENCE SUMMARY

(Erase heading not required.)

Army Form C. 2118

Place	Date	Hour	Summary of Events and Information	Remarks and references to Appendices
HANNESCAMPS	7/11/15		a sustained clear drone. It sounded very low, almost on the ground, & was followed by three loud reports, like those of a minenwerfer. The weather was misty so that nothing could be seen & investigations failed to trace the cause. Casualties: NIL. Enemy snipers were more active to-day, but without success. Two enemy shells landed on the parados & one on the parapet of T.65. No damage. Ten shells were sent about midday in the direction of HANNESCAMPS - BIENVILLERS road, but fell short. A strong fighting patrol went out at 5 P.M. in two parties, & under two officers, from T.64 & 65. They joined up in the open & advanced towards the old German trenches N. & S. of the ESSARTS road. Here they took up a position & lay in wait for the enemy parties, which frequently occupy these trenches; but nothing was either seen or heard. Casualties: NIL.	D.C. D.C.
HANNESCAMPS	8/11/15		Enemy snipers again active. The Battalion was relieved by the 6th Bedfordshire Regt; the first platoon entering at 5.10 P.M., & the relief being complete by 7 P.M. Work through the whole 6 days had been concentrated on the repair & drainage of trenches, which were left dry & in good condition, though much corduroy	D.C.

WAR DIARY
or
INTELLIGENCE SUMMARY

(Erase heading not required.)

Army Form C. 2118

Instructions regarding War Diaries and Intelligence Summaries are contained in F.S. Regs., Part II. and the Staff Manual respectively. Title Pages will be prepared in manuscript.

Place	Date	Hour	Summary of Events and Information	Remarks and references to Appendices
BIENVIL-LERS	9/11/15 to 14	—	will be needed before the mud is thoroughly got under. The Battalion returned to billets in BIENVILLERS. (~~crossed out~~) In billets:- battalion in reserve to the Brigade. Owing to the bad condition of the trenches, work was largely confined to repair of the sector rather than to the new work on VII Corps line. &c Relieved by 13th K.R.R. 14th	W.C. W.C.
HUMBERCAMP	14. 26/11/15 - 11/15		In billets: 112th Bde. in Reserve.	W.C.
BANNESCAMP	26/11/15		The Battalion relieved the 13th K.R.R.C; the first Platoon entering 4.10 P.M. Relief completed 5.29 P.M. The trenches were found to be in far better state than during the last tour of duty. Two of the communication trenches, however, CONDUIT AVENUE & CENTRAL AVENUE, were still water-logged. A great deal of trench-boarding had been put in position, & work was mainly devoted to sump-pits & repair of dug-outs, which suffered badly during the wet spell. By arrangement with O.C. 6th Bedfords, in reserve to the Brigade, that Battalion found daily a ration-party of 16 men for each of the Companies (except No 1, "O 6 Y".) This arrangement, which was mutual & permanent, set more men free for work & neutralized one of the disadvantages of having all 4 Companies in the trenches. The relief of No 1 Company was delayed ½ an hour owing to enemy shell-fire, which was also directed on No 4 Company while in BERLIN ST, but no dam-	W.C.

WAR DIARY
or
INTELLIGENCE SUMMARY
(Erase heading not required.)

Army Form C. 2118

Place	Date	Hour	Summary of Events and Information	Remarks and references to Appendices
ANNES- CAMPS.	27.11.15.		ase was done.— The enemy was unusually quiet. Casualties: NIL. With the exception of Artillery fire, everything was again very quiet, & a patrol which went out from T.66 at 4.30 P.M. saw & heard nothing of the enemy. A gun, which had been sending 77m. shells into the lines of No 1 Company, was reported by Capt. A. CALDICOTT to be at E.23.d.6.6. "B" Batt., 125th Bde R.F.A. was informed & opened fire, on which the German gun ceased fire. Sentries in No 2 Cy sector reported a noiseless rifle firing on more than one occasion from the direction of ESSARTS. Casualties: NIL. Wind: none. Frosty weather.	D.C.
HANNES- CAMPS.	28.11.15.		Enemy snipers were again less active, & a patrol for the second night in succession failed to see or hear any Germans. The line would seem to be held by a different Battalion from former tours of trenches. At midnight the enemy whist-led & shouted across humourous remarks in English. This had not been reported on former occasions, though singing had been heard. A German biplane which flew over our lines at 10 A.M. in the direction of FONQUEVILLERS, painted white & apparently quite new, closely resembled a Vickers fighting biplane. Casualties: NIL. Wind: none. Frosty weather.	D.C.

Army Form C. 2118

WAR DIARY
or
INTELLIGENCE SUMMARY
(Erase heading not required.)

Instructions regarding War Diaries and Intelligence Summaries are contained in F.S. Regs., Part II. and the Staff Manual respectively. Title Pages will be prepared in manuscript.

Place	Date	Hour	Summary of Events and Information	Remarks and references to Appendices
HANNES- CAMPS	29.11.15.	—	Under orders 112 Inf. Bde., a three-day relief within the Brigade was instituted for this sector, & the 6th Bedfords relieved; the 1st Company entering 4. to P.M. & the relief being completed by 6.5 P.M. A three days' hard frost was followed by thaw & rain & the trenches were left in a bad condition.	

STRENGTH: 30.11.15:
OFFICERS, 27; O.R., 945.

SICK DURING MONTH : " : " 30.
KILLED   " : " : " 4.
WOUNDED   " : " : " 4.
DIED OF WOUNDS " : " 1.
MISSING   " : " : " 2.
ACCIDENTALLY WOUNDED: OFFICERS, 1*; O.R., 3.

(* Lieut. J. GRAVETT, Grenade officer, wounded while instructing Grenadiers, 16.11.15, & sent to England.)

REINFORCEMENT: OFFICERS, 1§; O.R., Nil.
(§ 2nd Lieut. N. CHAMBERLAIN, from 11th (S) Bn loyal N. Lancs. Regt.)

Desmond Coke,
Capt. & Adjt.
1st L.N. Lancs. Rgt.

30.11.15.

112th Inf.Bde.
37th Div.

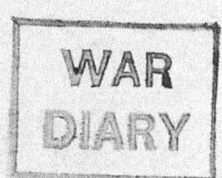

10th BATTN. THE LOYAL NORTH LANCASHIRE REGIMENT.

DECEMBER

1915

CONFIDENTIAL.

WAR DIARY.

10TH S. BN LOYAL N. LANCS RGT.

DEC. 1, 1915 — DEC. 31, 1915.

PART V.

INTELLIGENCE SUMMARY

(Erase heading not required.)

Place	Date	Hour	Summary of Events and Information	Remarks and references to Appendices
BIENVIL-LERS.	1 & 2/12/15	—	In billets at BIENVILLERS, as Battalion in reserve. Enemy artillery began during this period to devote attention to the 10th Battalion billeting area: particularly to "A" Coy. Mess + to Bn. Hd Qrs, which received a 77m. shell on the 2nd inst. No casualties. At 4.10 P.M. the relief of the 6th Bedford Regiment began + was completed by 7.30 P.M. The operation was much delayed by the bad state of the communication-trenches.	D.R.
HANNES-CAMPS.	3/12/15		The trenches were found to be in a worse condition than on any previous relief. The water had to a large extent been removed by means of trench pumps, but a thick adhesive mud made progress along the trenches everywhere difficult + in places impossible. Several men had to be dug out; more than one in an exhausted state. Work was devoted to clearing a way, as far as possible, at the worst points, + to repair of the fire-trenches. The enemy was quiet : but a patrol of 1 N.C.O. + 5 men, sent out from T.66 at 11.30 P.M. to ascertain the truth in a hypothesis that the enemy had withdrawn from their front line, found a large German working party at about E.18,0,7,4. Not a single round, however, was fired at T.66,67, or 68, between 9 P.M. on the 3rd + 10 A.M. on the fourth, so that the enemy may be presumed to have been engaged on the repair of their trenches.	D.C.

INTELLIGENCE SUMMARY

(Erase heading not required.)

Summaries are contained in F.S. Regs., Part II. and the Staff Manual respectively. Title Pages will be prepared in manuscript.

Place	Date	Hour	Summary of Events and Information	Remarks and references to Appendices
HANNES-CAMPS.	4. 12. 15.		Activity by our Artillery, 2.P.M. onwards, provoked retaliation. Only one shell, however, took effect: 5 men being wounded in T.63. by a 77 m.m. Work was again given up to the repair of trenches. Owing to the urgency of this & the scarcity of men for work, with all 4 Companies in the fire-trenches, it was thought inadvisable to send out patrols. The enemy was quiet: but the Signalling Sergeant was fired on by a machine-gun, whilst wiring, & seriously wounded.	A.C.
HANNES-CAMPS.	5. 12. 15.		The Battalion was relieved by the 6th Bedford Regt, the first Platoon leaving 4.10 P.M. & the relief being completed by 9.15 P.M. Owing to the state of the trenches, the relief was conducted for the most part overground. The Battalion went into billets at BIENVILLERS.	D.C.
BIENVIL-LERS	6-8. 12. 12. 15. 15.		Work-parties were found mainly for the fire-trenches. Enemy artillery again active on our billeting area: "A" Coy receiving the 4th shell on the 7th inst. 3 men wounded: (1 died of wounds) The Battalion was relieved by the 13 K.R.R.C. on the 8th inst: 5 P.M, & went into billets at HUMBERCAMPS.	A.C.

1875 Wt. W593/826 1,000,000 4/15 J.B.C. & A. A.D.S.S./Forms/C. 2118.

INTELLIGENCE SUMMARY

(Erase heading not required.)

Summaries are contained in F.S. Regs., Part II. and the Staff Manual respectively. Title Pages will be prepared in manuscript.

Place	Date	Hour	Summary of Events and Information	Remarks and references to Appendices
HUMBER-CAMPS.	20/12/15 — 8/12/15	—	In billets. Brigade in Reserve. Training of Bombers & reserve Machine Gunners carried on; also wire-breaking practice; & digging largely to fire-trenches of our sector. Capt. A. CALDICOTT (2nd-in-Command "B" Coy) was evacuated sick, 15th inst, + proceeded to England, 22nd. Col. N. DENNYS, (Gommels,) proceeded to England, 17.12.15, under orders from War Office. 2nd Lt. A.D. TEASDALE joined 8/12/15; 2nd Lt. T.T. WREN, 8/12/15; + 2nd Lt. E.C. WOOLLEY, 19/12/15.	D.C.
HANNES-CAMPS:	20 26/12 — 15/12/15	—	The Battalion relieved the 13th K.R.R.C., the first platoon entering at 3.30 P.M. + the relief being complete by 6.15 P.M. The trenches were found in a better condition than on the occasion of the last relief; No 4 Coy sector being almost normal + its communication trench, COLLINGBOURNE AVENUE, in fair condition. A new system of reliefs taken on from the 111th Bde, was adopted; the 4 Companies remaining in the trenches for 6 days, but 2 platoons of each Company being actually in the fire-trenches + 2 platoons in support bivouacs. These last had already been constructed by the 111th Bde from timber, canvas, corrugated iron, &c. :— as follows: (Ref 57. D. Map. N.E: 1/10,000) No 1 Coy: E 22.A.2.2. No 2 & 3: E 16.A.4.7. No 4: E 10.d.9.2.	D.C.

INTELLIGENCE SUMMARY

(Erase heading not required.)

Place	Date	Hour	Summary of Events and Information	Remarks and references to Appendices
			A system of 24-hour reliefs of half-companies was instituted, & worked successfully; no case of trench-foot occurring although phenomenally heavy rain began on the 21st, continuing at intervals until reliefs, & the trenches were very soon in a worse condition than on any previous occasion. Lateral communication along the fire-trench was interrupted at many points, & by Dec. 24 it was impossible to reach any Company without proceeding overground. Work was devoted to revetting, drainage, berms, & to the formation of new breastworks behind the original line of fire-trenches. Owing to the urgency of this work no large patrols were sent out, & the parties that patrolled in front of the various Company sectors nightly reported no enemy repair. Germans were seen proceeding overground, (on more than one occasion accounted for by Machine Gun or rapid fire,) & the condition of the enemy trenches probably accounted for enemy inactivity, which was so marked as to make a daily chronicle superfluous. German Artillery, however, was comparatively active during the whole period, but almost without exception the shells landed well behind the fire-	D.C.

INTELLIGENCE SUMMARY

(Erase heading not required.)

Place	Date	Hour	Summary of Events and Information	Remarks and references to Appendices
			bays, in the neighbourhood of the support-trenches. Casualties for the 6 days: Wounded in Action: Officers, Nil. O.R: 9. Killed " " " Nil. " " 1. Died of Wounds " " Nil. " " 1.	D.C.
			Major R.P. COBBOLD, 10th R. Fusiliers, assumed command of the Battalion, Dec. 25. Lt. † 9th LT. DEMPSTER was evacuated sick, Dec. 29. There was no fraternizing between the opposing forces on Christmas day. Our men showed their intention at dawn with machine gun + rapid rifle fire, + no enemy advances were observed thereafter. Sounds of singing + laughing were heard in the German trenches opposite No.1 Coy sector by patrols, 8-10 P.M. The Battalion was relieved on the 26th Dec. by the 6th Bn: Bedford Regt. + proceeded to BIENVILLERS, in reserve to the Brigade.	
BIENVILLERS	26-31/12/15	—	In billets. Work-parties were found daily for No 2 Bn: (holding the sector at HANNESCAMPS,) + the R.E. Wounded during digging-fatigue during this period: Officers, Nil; Other Ranks, 4.	D.C.
			STRENGTH, 31.12.15 — 29 Officers: O.R, 915. Sick to hospital during month — 2 Officers: O.R., 39. Killed during month:— Officers, Nil; O.R., 1.	

R.P. Cobbold
Capt. + Adjt, 10. L.N.L.
St. Colonel,
Commdg. 10th S. Bn:
Loyal N. Lancs. Regt.

112th Brigade.
37th Division.

1/10th LOYAL NORTH LANCASHIRE REGIMENT

JANUARY 1916

WAR DIARY
or
INTELLIGENCE SUMMARY

Army Form C. 2118

Ref^e 57^D : N.E. Sheets 1 & 2 [Pt 4]
1/10,000

(Erase heading not required.)

Place	Date	Hour	Summary of Events and Information	Remarks and references to Appendices
BIENVILLERS	1.1.16	3 P.M.	Battalion moved into billets at HUMBERCAMPS; 112th Bde. in Reserve.	D.C.
HUMBER-CAMPS.	1.1.16 –12.1.16.		In billets. The customary training was carried on, & digging on the Subsidiary Trench Line, &c.	D.C.
			2nd & 4th Lt^ DEMPSTER notified so do to England, 6.1.16.	
HANNES-CAMPS	13.1.16.	5.45 P.M.	The Battalion relieved the 13th K.R.R.C. in trenches: the first Platoon entering Companies had to proceed largely on top. The trenches were found in a better, though not in a good, condition. Trenches 68 & 59 were notably bad & impassable. The enemy showed unusual inactivity & were possibly also carrying out a relief. Capt. G.W. AINSWORTH evacuated sick.	D.C.
	14.1.16.		Enemy quiet except for occasional bursts of Machine Gun Fire, & hostile parties encountered by none of the patrols on the various Company fronts. A British aeroplane, which flew low over the Z', (E 23 c 7.6,) drew only three or four rounds of enemy rifle fire; but when it proceeded along the line Northwards, a heavy fusillade was opened & the line there seemed strongly held.	D.C.
	15.1.16.		Enemy machine-guns again active & heavy rifle-fire opposite N° 2 Company at morning stand-to. Patrols again heard & saw nothing of importance.	

WAR DIARY
or
INTELLIGENCE SUMMARY
(Erase heading not required.)

Instructions regarding War Diaries and Intelligence Summaries are contained in F.S. Regs., Part II. and the Staff Manual respectively. Title Pages will be prepared in manuscript.

Place	Date	Hour	Summary of Events and Information	Remarks and references to Appendices
	16.1.16.		During the day a dug-out of trenches each Company, under Brigade orders, constructed a dug-out to be used in the event of a bombardment. These works attracted a good deal of enemy artillery fire, but no real damage + no casualties resulted + the work in each case was carried through successfully. A new German 5.9. battery seems to have been installed behind G⁽ᵈᵉ⁾ FERME DU BOIS DU QUESNOY (about F.14.a.9.8.) where there was already a 77 m.m. gun; + fire was also directed for the first time on N° 4 C°⁽ʸ⁾ dug-out in Collingbourne Avenue (E.10.d.9.1.) from the direction of LA BRAYELLE. These are situated, facing S.W., in a steep bank + had been well protected from fire hitherto directed entirely from MONCHY + its neighbourhood. Considerable attention was devoted to the ground opposite N° 4 Company, including the Ravine, (E.11.c. – E.17.b.) as it was reported to be occupied by enemy patrols, who found cover in a hedge, marked X in the rough sketch (attached.) 2nd L⁴ ST. ANDREWES, B⁴ M.G.O., took out a patrol of 24 men with a machine-gun, 16.1.16, at dusk, covered by another machine-gun that enfiladed the bank (Y) from Trench 67. The disused trench was occupied + the hedge made good in advance by 4 men who crawled out at 3 P.M. The light ex-	D.C. See PLAN.1.

WAR DIARY
or
INTELLIGENCE SUMMARY

(Erase heading not required.)

Instructions regarding War Diaries and Intelligence Summaries are contained in F. S. Regs., Part II. and the Staff Manual respectively. Title Pages will be prepared in manuscript.

Place	Date	Hour	Summary of Events and Information	Remarks and references to Appendices
			abled one of these men, Pte FLETCHER, J., (N° 14156.) to give useful information as to distances &c. These were later resified by 2nd Lt. ANDREWS, who took compass bearings & made a plan of the Ravine (attached.) ~~Towards~~ Pte FLETCHER also reported two German saps at 80 yds distance from their wire; their heads protected by a circle of barbed wire. The bank was found to be lined with snipers' pits & cuts, giving excellent cover for sniping on our lines. The 4 men in advance were apparently observed by the enemy, as a party of bombers crawled towards them shortly after dusk; on being fired at, withdrew to the BANK, from which rapid fire was opened & a Very light sent up by another hostile party. 2nd Lt. ANDREWS opened fire with the machine-gun, as 20 Germans came over the skyline at the double *in open order, apparently with effect, as cheers were heard & one man was seen being supported as the party retired. Lights were now going up from every direction & the enemy seemed thoroughly alarmed, so that 2nd Lt. ANDREWS decided to withdraw the patrol into our own lines, which he effected without casualties.	see Plan 2. D.C.
	17.4.16.		A concentrated machine-gun fire demonstration against MONCHY by the 110th Inf. Bde., at 6.40 P.M. & after, drew no retaliation on this sector; but after the first burst of fire a group of 3 green rockets went up from the trenches	

INTELLIGENCE SUMMARY
or

(Erase heading not required.)

Instructions regarding War Diaries and Intelligence Summaries are contained in F. S. Regs., Part II. and the Staff Manual respectively. Title Pages will be prepared in manuscript.

Place	Date	Hour	Summary of Events and Information	Remarks and references to Appendices
HANNES-CAMPS.	18.1.16		In front of TONCHY + similar groups were sent up frequently till 7.30 P.M., extending as far South as E 23 d. Since no recall followed, the signal was presumably an alarm. Patrols met no enemy parties.	DC
			Enemy machine-guns active. Otherwise a quiet day. 2nd Lt. ANDREWS went out with a machine-gun to a patrol of 41 Other Ranks, hoping to engage the enemy in the RAVINE, but no party was encountered; 1st + no.1 + 2 Coy. patrols reported all quiet. Opposite no. 1 Coy, a German shouted "Now, Tommies," about 10 P.M. + this was immediately followed by enemy Machine-Gun fire.	DC
	19.1.16	5 P.M	The Bn. was relieved by 6th Bedfordshire Regt.	DC
BIENVIL-LERS.	19.1.-25.1.16.		Major A. McC. WEBSTER, 2nd in Command, evacuated sick. Battalion in Reserve. Digging fatigues as usual.	
HUMBER-CAMPS.	25.1.-31.		In billets : 113th Bde in Reserve. 2nd Lt. N. CHAMBERLAIN proceeded to England, 26.1.16, with orders to report in writing to the War Office.	

Strength : Officers, 27. ; O.R. , 870.

Sick during month : O,3 ; O.R., 52.

Killed in Action. O. Nil : O.R. —
Wounded " : O. — ; O.R. 4.
Accidental wounds, O, — ; O.R. 1.
Died. ?

Desmond Coke.
Capt. & Adjt.

McPherson Major,
For O.C. 10 L.N. Lancs. Regt.

Instructions regarding War Diaries and Intelligence Summaries are contained in F.S. Regs., Part II. and the Staff Manual respectively. Title Pages will be prepared in manuscript.

INTELLIGENCE SUMMARY
or
(Erase heading not required.)

Place	Date	Hour	Summary of Events and Information	Remarks and references to Appendices
			ROUGH SKETCH OF RAVINE.	COPY OF 2nd LE ANDREWS' PLAN.

A : Lone Tree.
B.C : Bank.
D.E : Oseraie.
F.H : Hedge (+ Bank.)

DISTANCES:
T.66 – A : 200 yds.
T.66 – B : 450 "
B – C : 200 "
D – E : 200 "
F – H : 330 "
A – F : 320 "

CONTOUR as shown in Map 57 D; 1/10,000.
———— 2nd LE ANDREWS's
- - - - - - - - - collected.

1875. Wt. W593/826 1,000,000 4/15 J.B.C. & A. A.D.S.S./Forms/C. 2118.

Instructions regarding War Diaries and Intelligence Summaries are contained in F.S. Regs., Part II. and the Staff Manual respectively. Title Pages will be prepared in manuscript.

INTELLIGENCE SUMMARY

or

Summary of Events and Information

(Erase heading not required.)

Place	Date	Hour	Nº 3 Bⁿ (11ᵗʰ R. Warwick.)	Nº 2 Bⁿ (10 L.N.L.) (in Bedford Bgd.)	Nº 1 Bⁿ (8ᵗʰ E. LANCS)	Remarks and references to Appendices

Coy Nº:

8 7 6 5 ← 4 → 3 2 1

Companies from the Right.

C/125 shoots over 110ᵗʰ Bde. Area.

D.C.

CHART of REVISED CONNECTIONS WITH R.F.A.

112ᵗʰ bde (& 111 d.)

112th Brigade.
37th Division.

1/10th LOYAL NORTH LANCASHIRE REGIMENT

FEBRUARY 1 9 1 6

WAR DIARY / INTELLIGENCE SUMMARY

Army Form C. 2118

Place	Date	Hour	Summary of Events and Information	Remarks and references to Appendices
HOMBER CAMP.	1.2.16	—	In billets. Divisional Reserve.	D.C.
ANNES-CAMP.	6.2.16	—	Battalion relieved the 13th K.R.R.C.; first platoon entering 6.15 P.M. & the relief being complete 8.30 P.M. The trenches were found in good order; COLLINGBOURNE AV., CHISWICK AV., & CRAWLBOYS LANE, allowing the relief to take place in communication trenches. Part of T.59 was still impassable. The enemy were quiet, & patrols had nothing to report.	D.C.
"	7.2.16		Enemy Artillery active. The half-completed dug-out in LANDLEAGUE AV. attracted a good deal of the fire, being in white chalk. 20 shells, 77 m.m., fell in its immediate neighbourhood between 12 noon & 4 P.M., but no damage was done. This dug-out has some 15 ft. of earth above its roof, being tunnelled, & is intended as a shelter in case of heavy bombardment. Three shells out of six directed on the Aufsort Bivouacs of No 2 Coy were blinds. Patrols again met no hostile parties.	D.C.
"	8.2.16		The activity of enemy Artillery was again noticeable. 50 rounds, 4.9. HOWITZER, were fired at 10 G.A.M. onwards, on the line from E 21.	D.C.

WAR DIARY
or
INTELLIGENCE SUMMARY
(Erase heading not required.)

Army Form C. 2118

Place	Date	Hour	Summary of Events and Information	Remarks and references to Appendices
HANNES-CAMPS.	9.2.16.		b.5.7. to E.21.d.6.0. (orchards &c.) & there was general liveliness on both sides over a large area: our Artillery carrying out a combined bombardment of "She 2": (E.23.c.) from 8 P.M. till 12.20 An Officer patrol, which lay out in the Ravine, from 8 P.M. till 12.20 A.M. saw & heard no enemy parties about. Orders received from 112 Inf. Bde re re-distribution of line as follows: 37ᵗʰ GD.W! Line: The present front of the 110ᵗʰ Bde to become the Right Sector & to be increased by a sector now held by three French Companies. This RIGHT SECTOR to be held, as follows, alternately by 110ᵗʰ & 112ᵗʰ Bde, in reliefs: (1) Right D!: Trench. 77 - 88 (incl.) (2) R. Centre: " 89 - 96 (") (3) Left " : " 97 - 105 (") (4) Left B!: = New French Trenches (Northernmost point: W.17.d.8.6) The 112ᵗʰ Bde will hold this frontage as follows: (1) 6ᵗʰ Bedfords ; (2) 10 L.N.L. (3) 8ᵗʰ E. Lancs. (4) 11ᵗʰ R. Warwicks; proceeding, when the Bde is in Divisional Reserve, to billets as follows: (1) BIENVILLERS, (2) HUMBERCAMPS (old billets) (3) POMMIER = (4) ST AMAND: (old billets.) The LEFT SECTOR, extending from left of Right Sector, to	Refce Map 57 D N.E 1 & 2.8.4. OS: 1/10000 D.C. D.C.

WAR DIARY or INTELLIGENCE SUMMARY

Army Form C. 2118

Place	Date	Hour	Summary of Events and Information	Remarks and references to Appendices
			about X.1.a.6.1, will be held permanently by 111th B'de: 2 Co'ys in trenches & 2 in B'de Reserve.	
			Under this scheme the Co'ys disposition will be as follows:	
			BN H.Q: STONEYGATE ST., temporarily (see below x)	
			2 Co'ys: Front trenches.	
			1 Coy: BIENVILLERS until Div'l 2nd line is ready: then 2, 3, + Support B'i.	D.C.
			1 Coy: BIENVILLERS, pending construction of B'y dug-outs + R't H.Q.x in a new communication trench to be made from junction of Support Line (W.28.d.9.9) round to BIENVILLERS, when the 2 rear Co'ys more up one place.	
			The portion of the line at present held by the Right B'de of the 39th Div'n: will be taken over by the 48th DIVN.	
			"	
			The day's activity was again confined chiefly to Artillery fire, which was heavy on both sides; to aerial skirmishes. 200 rounds — 77 m.m, 4.5, & 5.9, — were fired into FONQUEVILLERS during the afternoon.	
			The night was fine & frosty, but 4 officer patrols failed to find any German out on the Battalion front.	

WAR DIARY
INTELLIGENCE SUMMARY

Army Form C. 2118

Place	Date	Hour	Summary of Events and Information	Remarks and references to Appendices
HANNES-CAMPS.	10.2.16.		Artillery & aircraft again active. Forty 5.9 shells were sent into our lines, without doing any damage. Of these, 15 were blind. Six 77 m.m. shells landed near Hd Qrs, & there was general liveliness over a wide area.	D.C.
BIENVIL-LERS.	10.2.16 to 13.		The Battalion was relieved by the 6th Bedfordshire Regt. & proceeded into B'de Reserve at BIENVILLERS. In billets. Issue of standed orders re billets when B'de is in Divisional Reserve: (16.7. x 6/9, 10/2/16, cancelling 16.4. x 674:) — i.e. 11th Bn R. Warwick Regt. — HUMBERCAMP. 8th E. Lancs Regt. — " 6th Bedford Regt. — ST AMAND. 10th L.N. Lancs. Regt — POMMIER. The disposition in the lines remains unaltered: N° 1 B'n, 6th Bedfords; N° 2 B'n, 10th L.N. Lancs; N° 3 B'n, 8th E. Lancs; N° 4 B'n, 11th R. Warwick (numbering from the Right.)	D.C.
POMMIER.	13.2.16 to 18.2.16.		In billets. B'de in Divisional Reserve. Working parties were sent up to the proposed N° Hd Qrs, where dug-outs were begun. The billets occupied were those vacated by two Companies of the 3rd (Pioneer) B'n N.Stafford Regt. & various details.	D.C.

WAR DIARY or INTELLIGENCE SUMMARY

Army Form C. 2118

Place	Date	Hour	Summary of Events and Information	Remarks and references to Appendices
RAVINE.	16.2.16.		The Battalion relieved the 7th Bn. Leicester Regt. in trenches; the line of trenches running from T.83 (on the MONCHY-BIENVILLERS Road) to T.96 at about 29.A.7.5. (Ref. to Map 51c, S.E. 3 & 4, part of.) Right Sector: 89 to the MONCHY-BERLES Road in T.92. Left Sector: this road to T.96. The disposition of Companies was: Right Sector, D Coy. (to be relieved by B Coy.) Left Sector, C Coy. (to be relieved by A Coy.) A & B Coy being temporarily in BIENVILLERS. Artillery connections: Right Sector, D.124: Left Sector, C.185. The trenches were found in a damp condition, owing to continued rain, & the Beaumans, who were observed to be busy baling, were unusually quiet.	D.C.
" "	17.2.16.		Enemy again exceptionally quiet. A few rifle grenades were thrown over at points where the trenches run nearest to the Germans. The nearest point, 35 yards, is at Trench 95. Three of eight 4.2 shells directed on T.93 were blind.	D.C.
" "	18.2.16.		Enemy again inactive & heard baling.	D.C.
" "	19.2.16.		A clear frosty day, after rain, revived aerial activity. An enemy airship or very powerful aeroplane was over our sector, 10.45 P.M. to 11.30 P.M., & dropped bombs in the direction of HANNESCAMPS. The noise was big, but though the night was very light, nothing could be seen. D.C.	D.C.

WAR DIARY
or
INTELLIGENCE SUMMARY
(Erase heading not required.)

Army Form C. 2118

Place	Date	Hour	Summary of Events and Information	Remarks and references to Appendices
RAVINE.	20.2.16.		At 7.50 A.M. five British aeroplanes passed over our front at 7.50 A.M. flying in a North Easterly direction under heavy enemy fire. The enemy rifle again quiet, + of the few 4.2 shells fired about 33% were blind. The construction of a system of concealed sniping posts along our front was to-day concluded.	D.C.
"	21.2.16.		A quiet day.	D.C.
"	22.2.16.		At 10.45 A.M. three 77 m.m. shells were sent on to a point about 20 yards west of Bn. Hd Qrs. These were the first shells directed on this front of the RAVINE since the commencement of the dug-outs for Bn. in Support + Hd Qr details; a no damage was done.	D.C.
Pernois	23.2.16		Billets:- Bde in Divisional reserve. Arrived in rest billets about 9.30 p.m. on the 22nd Feb: I took over billets vacated by the 4th Leicesters. Each day a digging party of 100 of 2 Officers is sent up to carry on with new dug-outs in Ravine for Battn Hd Qrs + 1 Company in reserve. Various other digging parties are sent out each day. All leaves cancelled until	S.H. S.H. S.H.

1375 Wt. W593/826 1,000,000 4/15 J.B.C. & A. A.D.S.S./Forms/C. 2118.

WAR DIARY or INTELLIGENCE SUMMARY

Army Form C. 2118

Place	Date	Hour	Summary of Events and Information	Remarks and references to Appendices
POMMIER	23.2.16		Further orders.	S/A
	24.2.16		Nil.	S/A
	25.2.16		Nil.	S/A
	26.2.16		Nil.	S/A
	27.2.16		Working parties all day clearing roads from snow etc.	
	28.2.16		Nil	
HANNESCAMP	29.2.16		At 7pm the Battalion relieved the 8th Leicesters R/C. Our line was Trench 58 — Trench 65 inclusive. Two Coys in the line & two in support at Hannescamp. The 10th L.N. Lancs is the right battalion of the 112th Bde. 8th East Lancs relieving in enemy 6 days. The relief was completed at 1.45 p.m. without any accident. 2nd Lieut N. H. Chamberlain - relinquished his commission - Feb 20th. E.Howell Strength: Officers 29, O.R. 862	Killed in action 0 Nil. O.R. Lt/Adjt 5 Pte R/C 10th L.N. Lancs Wounded 0, 2 5 or 1. R 1.3.16 Accidental killed 0, 1. O.R.O 1.3.16 Died. 0, 1. O.R. 46

112th Brigade.
37th Division.

1/10th LOYAL NORTH LANCASHIRE REGIMENT

MARCH 1916

WAR DIARY
INTELLIGENCE SUMMARY
(Erase heading not required.)

Army Form C. 2118

Place	Date	Hour	Summary of Events and Information	Remarks and references to Appendices
Hammes camp	1.3.16		The Battalion relieved the 8th Worcester Reg. (144 Bde) in trenches. The line held is T56 - T66 (inclusive), leaving 2 Coys in front line & 2 Companies in Support. The Communication trenches were found in a bad condition also the left Sector that is T63-T66 were not good. Enemy exceptionally quiet.	S/L 2/L S/L
"	2.3.16		Enemy very quiet except for bursts of machine-gun fire at times. During the morning a B2 aeroplane flew along (very low) over our trenches, this seemed to annoy the enemy as they opened rapid fire & Machine Gun fire. Eventually the enemy became so desperate that they opened fire with field guns! All shots fires were very wide of their mark. Enemy still very quiet.	2/L S/L 2/L
"	3.3.16			2/L
"	4.3.16		Patrol went out under Lieut Squibb, but nothing was heard or seen of the enemy.	2/L

WAR DIARY
or
INTELLIGENCE SUMMARY
(Erase heading not required.)

Army Form C. 2118

Place	Date	Hour	Summary of Events and Information	Remarks and references to Appendices
HANNES-CAMPS.	5.3.16.		Enemy again quiet. A powerful searchlight was in action, 9.20 - 9.40 P.M.; apparently from a point about E.23.d.1.2; lighting up our trenches & those of the enemy as well. No action followed. The German trenches appeared in bad condition, as they frequently exposed & offered good targets to our snipers. Six 77 M.M. shells fired at 10 A.M. on CHISWICK AV. only one exploded. Our Lewis Guns fired on the ESSARTS RD. during the night.	D.C.
HANNES-CAMPS.	6.3.16.		The Battalion was relieved by the 8th Bn. East Lancashire Regt. & proceeded into billets at BIENVILLERS, in support, as N° 3 Bn.	
BIENVIL-LERS.	7.3.16.		Orders received as to extension of the right of the Brigade to Trench 50 (inclusive) on 8th inst. This had hitherto been T.58. The movement to be effected as follows: N° 2 (B"), Left, to extend its right to T. 64 : N° 1 (Right) No 1 + No 2 B"s to have 3 Companies each in the front line & one in Support at FONQUEVILLERS & HANNESCAMPS respectively. Hd Qrs to be in these villages. Hd Qrs of N° 3 B" to Remain at BIENVILLERS, with 2 Coys at HANNESCAMPS & 2 at FONQUEVILLERS. Hd Qrs of N° 4 B" at POMMIER, with 4 Companies there resting.	

WAR DIARY or INTELLIGENCE SUMMARY

Army Form C. 2118

Place	Date	Hour	Summary of Events and Information	Remarks and references to Appendices
BIENVIL- LERS. NO.3 B.N	6.3.16. 8-12th 3.16		The 8th East Lancashire Regt. & 10th R.N. Lancs Regt. will alternate as No. 1 B.N. The 6th Bedford Regt. & 11 R. Warwick Regt. as No. 2 B.N.; each Batt'n becoming No. 3 & No. 4 one time in four. B'DE HD QRS: BIENVILLERS. Batt'e Post: E.g.a.5.1. No.1 B.N to hold T. 50-63; No.2 to hold 64-77; No.3 B'n to be earmarked for the defence of the Div. 2nd line; No.4 to be at the disposal of the B.G.C. 11th B'de; in the event of an Alarm. The B'de Machine Gun Company having arrived, Lewis Gun detachments to be at the disposal of O.C. No 1 & 2 B'ns: those of No.3 being divided between the FONQUEVILLERS & HANNESCAMPS detachments. Movement as above carried out. Detachments employed in all-night shifts mining the NORTH & SOUTH FORTIN, the former having been the objective of a hostile raid whilst held by the 48th Div.	D.C.
FONQUE- VILLERS.	12. 3.16.		The Battalion relieved the 8th B'n E. Lancs. Regt. as No. 1 B'n in Trenches, with Hd Qrs at FONQUEVILLERS. 2nd Lt. ANDREWS returned to duty after ab-sence sick. Present disposition of B'DE: No 1 B'n, 10 L.N. Lancs R.; No 2, 11th R. Warwicks Regt. (Hd Qrs, HANNESCAMPS); No 3 B'n, 6th Bedford Regt.; No 4 B'n, 8th East Lancs Regt. the Batt'n thus having the 11th R. Warwicks on its left & on its right the boundary between 3rd & 4th Armies.	D.C.

Army Form C. 2118

Instructions regarding War Diaries and Intelligence Summaries are contained in F. S. Regs., Part II. and the Staff Manual respectively. Title Pages will be prepared in manuscript.

WAR DIARY
or
INTELLIGENCE SUMMARY
(Erase heading not required.)

Place	Date	Hour	Summary of Events and Information	Remarks and references to Appendices
FONQUE-VILLERS.	13.3.16.		Artillery Support: T. 50-56, B/125; T. 57-63, D/125. Enemy Artillery quiet, but machine guns from N.W. corner of GOMMECOURT WOOD extremely active.	D.C.
"			Enemy Grenades, brought in from opposite the NORTH FORTIN, were found to be dated Jan. 12. 1916.	D.C.
"	14.3.16.		Enemy Artillery active: FONQUEVILLERS (Hd Qrs, &c.) being shelled during the day, + a bombardment of the approaches to the village taking place between 6.30 + 9.0 P.M. The SOUASTRE + BIENVILLERS roads were both thoroughly searched, with an intermittent shelling, at times very heavy, but the Regimental Transport got up, with some narrow escapes, + no damage resulted. This demonstration was taken to be retaliation for the 110th O'de shelling of German trenches near MONCHY, the night before.	D.C.
			Three men in these 2 days were hit by bullets on the shrapnel helmet + not injured.	
			The Lewis Guns of the Right Company fired at intervals on the GOMMECOURT-ESSARTS ROAD, where sounds were heard as of a relief.	

Army Form C. 2118

WAR DIARY
or
INTELLIGENCE SUMMARY
(Erase heading not required.)

Instructions regarding War Diaries and Intelligence Summaries are contained in F.S. Regs., Part II. and the Staff Manual respectively. Title Pages will be prepared in manuscript.

Place	Date	Hour	Summary of Events and Information	Remarks and references to Appendices
FONQUE-VILLERS	15.3.16.		An Officer patrol reported the German sentries to be very noisy & — from their voices — mostly young. 2nd & JUDE joined.	
" "	16.3.16.		Enemy Artillery again active, on targets widely distributed, throughout the day. A big proportion — probably 25% — were blind. The enemy were suspected of registering, possibly after a relief of batteries. Enemy still registering, notably on T. 56.57 & the 2nd & 3rd divisional lines. Artillery otherwise less active. Unusually heavy transport, the quietness of the enemy after a certain activity, the sounds of men singing on the march, & shorter shifts by German wiring-parties, all seemed to point to a relief on a big scale.	D.C. D.C.
" "	17.3.16.		Enemy again quiet. A German helmet, found in front of the North FORTIN, bore the number 170 as well as 119 R.; the name FUCHS; +under the badge, FURCHTLOS UND TREU: 170 being a Baden Reg. & 119 R. a regiment of the Reserve.	D.C.
" "	18.3.16.		Great use was made, during this period in trenches, of the telescopic rifles, & the Battalion snipers, by means of carefully constructed sniping-posts,	

Army Form C. 2118

WAR DIARY
or
INTELLIGENCE SUMMARY
(Erase heading not required.)

Instructions regarding War Diaries and Intelligence Summaries are contained in F.S. Regs., Part II. and the Staff Manual respectively. Title Pages will be prepared in manuscript.

Place	Date	Hour	Summary of Events and Information	Remarks and references to Appendices
POMMIER.	19.3.16		behind the firing-line, have undoubtedly accounted for several of the enemy & have succeeded in repressing the activity of enemy snipers. 2nd Lt. SQUIBS has been responsible for their training. The Battalion was relieved by the 1st Bn East Lancs Regt., on the 4th G.W.R: taking over the line from the 27th G.W.R:, which was taken out of trenches for a rest: the 110th & 111th Brigades going back to the neighbourhood of DOULLENS & MONDICOURT, the 112th returning temporarily to its former billets as Bde in Reserve, so soon as these billets were vacated by Units of the 4th Division. The Bn marched to POMMIER on relief, in billets.	D.C.
HUMBER- CAMPS.	20.3.16 - 31.3.16.	9 A.M.	The Battalion marched to its former billets. Digging on Corps line; inspections &c. The Commander-in-Chief visited the Area, 29.3.16, & rode round billets. 2nd Lt. DANE & ALLEN joined 26.3.16. Lt. GRAVETT, J.A, rejoined same day.	D.C.

Strength: Officers: 33.
Other Ranks: 894.

Killed in Action: 1.
Wounded: 5.
Died of Wounds: 1.

R. Cotton
Lieut-Colonel,
Commdg. 10th (S) Bn
Loyal N. Lancs. Regt.

112th Brigade.
37th Division.

1/10th LOYAL NORTH LANCASHIRE REGIMENT

APRIL 1916

WAR DIARY or INTELLIGENCE SUMMARY

Army Form C. 2118

(Erase heading not required.)

Place	Date	Hour	Summary of Events and Information	Remarks and references to Appendices
HUMBER-CAMPS	1-4-16		In billets. Digging on Corps Line; inspections &c.	
	8-4-16		Division inspected the Battalion on 1-4-16. Lt. & Q. Mr. Lee joined the Battalion for duty 1-4-16. Draft of 139 N.C.Os & men joined on 3-4-16.	P.B.
WARLUZEL	9.4.16	12 A.M.	The Battalion marched into WARLUZEL after being relieved by the 6th Leicesters. Billets were taken over from the 8th Leicesters and the Battalion commenced its period of rest having spent almost 4 months in the trenches.	P.B.
"	"	6 p.m.	Draft of 19 N.C.Os & men joined the Battalion	P.B.
"	" 23.	—	In billets. Company Training & fatigues.	D.C.
"	" 25.	—	2nd Lt. C.T. ROSTRON joined for duty.	D.C.
"	" 30.	—	Orders received from 112th Inf. Bde to be prepared to move at 9 A.M. 1.5.16.	D.C.

G. Cake,
Capt. & Adjt.
for O.C. 10 L.N. Lanc. Regt.

20-5-16.

112th Brigade.
37th Division.

1/10th LOYAL NORTH LANCASHIRE REGIMENT

M A Y 1 9 1 6

INTELLIGENCE SUMMARY

(Erase heading not required.)

Summaries are continued in F.S. Regs., Part II. and the Staff Manual respectively. Title Pages will be prepared in manuscript.

Place	Date	Hour	Summary of Events and Information	Remarks and references to Appendices
WARLUZEL	1.5.16	9 A.M.	The 37th Division having received orders to relieve the 4th Division in the trenches, the Battalion left WARLUZEL and marched into billets at POMMIER, arriving there at 12.30 noon.	PPB/-
POMMIER	2.5.16	9 P.M.	Orders received for the Btn. to relieve the 1st HAMPSHIRE Regt in the support trenches. Bttn Hd. Qrs. left POMMIER at 8.30 P.M. and took over Btn. Hd. Qrs. of the 1st Hampshires at BIENVILLERS at 9 P.M. The right detachment of the Battalion consisting of A & B Companies under Capt. R.M. DENNYS marched to FONQUEVILLERS and relieved A & D Companies of the 1st Hampshires at 10.30 P.M. and remained in close support to the 8th EAST. LANCASHIRES. The left detachment consisting of C & D Companies under Capt. J.B. DRYDEN marched to HANNESCAMPS and relieved B & C Companies of the 1st Hampshires & remained in close support to the 11th ROYAL WARWICKSHIRES.	
BIENVILLERS	3.5.16		A re-adjustment of the Brigade line was ordered as follows:— No 1. (Right) Btn. 8th EAST LANCS. - Trenches 50-59. Two Companies in front line trenches & two Companies in close support, one Coy at SNIPER'S SQUARE and Company in FONQUEVILLERS. No 2. (Centre) Btn. 11th ROYAL WARWICKS. Trenches 60-61. Two Companies in front line trenches and two Companies	PPB/-

INTELLIGENCE SUMMARY

(Erase heading not required.)

Place	Date	Hour	Summary of Events and Information	Remarks and references to Appendices
BIENVILLERS	3.5.16		in close support at HANNESCAMPS. No. 3 (Left) Btn. 6th BEDFORDS. Trenches 92 - 92. Four Companies in front line. No. 4 (Reserve) Btn. 10th LOYAL N. LANCS. at BIENVILLERS. At night are C.O.Y. of the Reserve Btn. to be in close support to No. 3. Btn. divided between trenches on HANNESCAMPS - MONCHY Road and support line behind the MONCHY Salient.	9AB
		8.30 P.M.	Btn. Hd. Qrs of the 6th BEDFORDS taken over at 8.30 p.m. Companies of the 8th EAST LANCS. relieved our night detachment which marched into BIENVILLERS into billets. The supporting Companies of the 11th ROYAL WARWICKS relieved our left detachment, & D Company marched into billets at BIENVILLERS - "C" Company moving into close support trenches behind MONCHY Salient. Relief completed at 10.30 p.m.	
"	4.5.16	2.30 A.M.	Enemy heavily bombarded the whole Divison Front & concentrated on the MONCHY Salient: & ultimately raided the trenches Nos. 79 & 82 which run front of the Salient. The two platoons of the supporting Company sustained casualties:- KILLED. 2nd LT. J.R. O'KEEFFE and one O.R. WOUNDED. 11 O.R.	9AB
		3.30		
"	5.5.16	8 A.M.	In billets. Usual working parties & found for Btns in front line. Two other trench casualties - shell wounds.	9B
		3 P.M.	Enemy shelled BIENVILLERS with 4.2 Howitzers. Some damage was done & one man buried in a shelter through a shell explosion, was "gassed".	

INTELLIGENCE SUMMARY

(Erase heading not required.)

Place	Date	Hour	Summary of Events and Information	Remarks and references to Appendices
BIENVILLERS	5-5-16		Special mention is made of No. 14424 SGT. RILEY. J. During the bombardment of BIENVILLERS nine men were buried in a cellar. SGT. RILEY immediately organised a rescue party & himself located the men buried in the cellar. Since he was overcome with fumes of the shell but he entered the cellar a third time & was entirely overcome by the fumes and had to be taken to hospital. Three of the men were dead and 6 wounded, but all were quickly liberated owing to the prompt action of SGT. RILEY. No. 13529. SGT. BROMLEY. T. No. 13802 LEE-SGT. REES. H & No. 15516 PTE. TUNSTALL. J. all rendered prompt and valuable assistance in Lillers.	99/-
"	6.5.16 to 8.5.16	noon	Working parties supplied to Battalions in front line trenches. Also a party of 50 men worked continuously night and day in tunnel leading to and from Bole Battle Headquarters. The Battalion relieved the 6th Bedford Regt. the first platoon entering at 8 p.m. and relief was complete by 9.30 p.m. Everything was very quiet. One man accidentally wounded.	99/-
Trenches.	9.5.16		Enemy was busy with trench mortar bombs and rifle grenades, but no damage was sustained by the Battalion.	
"	10.5.16		Orders received to hand over to the 8th EAST LANCASHIRES Trenches Y2 to Y7 inclusive, the dispositions of the Battalion were altered & the line held as follows:-	

1875 Wt. W593/826 1,000,000 4/15 J.B.C. & A. A.D.S.S./Forms/C. 2118.

Place	Date	Hour	Summary of Events and Information	Remarks and references to Appendices
Trenches	10.5.16		From right to left. B. Coy. Trenches 78 to 83 inclusive; C. Coy. Trenches 84 to 86 inclusive; A. Coy. Trenches 87 to 90 inclusive and D. Coy. Trenches 91 and 92. B. & D. Companies each had 3 Platoons in the fire trenches and one Platoon in support trenches. These dispositions allowed for the MONCHY SALIENT to be manned one Company. Change effected by 6 p.m. Enemy artillery was very quiet but rifle grenades and trench mortars caused us some trouble. One rifle grenade fell amongst a group of nine men, killing two and wounding six. Otherwise no casualties. Much work was needed in the trenches and as many unknown parties were about the trenches day and night, very little retaliation by us was carried out.	
	11.5.16		Enemy quiet. Trenches strengthened and improved.	P.B.
	12.5.16		Very few shells fired at the trenches, and generally everything was quiet. Trenches still improved.	P.B. P.B.
	13.5.16		Frequent exchange of bombs + rifle grenades took place during the day. Much attention paid to the construction of snipers posts, catapult emplacements etc. in order to obtain a sure footing and beat down the enemy's sniping + bombing	
	14.5.16		A very quiet day. The Battalion was relieved in the trenches by the	P.B.

Place	Date	Hour	Summary of Events and Information	Remarks and references to Appendices
Lucheux	14.5.16		6" Leicester Regt. The first platoon entering trenches at 9 p.m. Relief completed by 11 p.m. The Battalion proceeded to SAULTY and took over reserve billets from the 9th Leicester Regt. arriving at SAULTY	
Saulty	15.5.16	2.30 a.m. 15.5.16.	2. Lt. GOODMAN C.A. joined the Battalion for duty.	JK.
	16.5.16		Various digging parties were found for a new Railway (light line) which is being constructed between Halvet - Saulty to Bienvillers. So great a number of men were needed for this work that the Battalion training ceased to exist.	JK.
	17.5.16		N.1.	JK.
	18.5.16 –26.5.16		N.1. Detachment of 2 Companies sent to Bienvillers, and a working party for the M.O. by 15 Oct. This detachment was commanded by Capt. DENNYS. The Battalion relieved the 6 Leicester in support trenches at Bienvillers. The first platoon of the 10th N.L. arrived in Bienvillers about 10.50 pm. The relief being complete by 12 M.N.	JK.
Bienvillers	26.5.16		A large working party was required to dig a main trench line in advance of T59 – T63. This was completed in one night making the communication trench leading from the original front line to the	JK.

Place	Date	Hour	Summary of Events and Information	Remarks and references to Appendices
Beuvières	27.5.16		New front line. April T74 we had a wiring party of 30 men and 1 N.C.O. unfortunately just as they had finished & were about to return to the trench the enemy sent a salvo of whizz bangs over in conjunction with a salvo of 4.2 Shrapnel, one man was killed and two others wounded slightly.	2/t
"	28.5.16		300 men are out each night carrying out advanced front line.	2/t
"	29.5.16		The enemy shelled Beuvières slightly causing 6 casualties among	2/t
"	30.5.16		The Artillery - though none of our men were hit.	2/t
"	31.5.16		Nil.	

Strength: Officers 33
Other ranks 946

Killed in Action: 1 officer and 4 other ranks.
Wounded: 27 (including 5 slightly wounded at duty)
Died of wounds: Nil.
Self inflicted wounds: One.
Suffering from gas effects. One.

E. Howell
Lieut & Adjt.
for O.C. 10th Loyal North Lancs Regt.

112th Brigade.
37th Division.

Attached to 34th Division from 5th July
to 21st August 1916;

1/10th BATTALION

LOYAL NORTH LANCASHIRE REGIMENT

JUNE 1916:

INTELLIGENCE SUMMARY

Vol XI

(Erase heading not required.)

Place	Date	Hour	Summary of Events and Information	Remarks and references to Appendices
Bienvillers	1.6.16	9 A.M.	All working parties ceased at 12 m.d. At 7.30 the right Company (B Coy) of the 10th L.N. Lanes left Bienvillers and relieved the Right Coy of the Bedfords (6th) in the trenches. The other three Coys followed at 10 minute intervals and the relief was complete at 10 p.m.	E/H
Trenches	2.6.16		First night passed quietly. This morning at Stand-to two men of B Coy were slightly wounded by a rifle grenade. Our snipers have so far accounted for over 4 periscopes & 2 Germans.	S/H O/H
	3.6.16		At 3.30 p.m. after a very quiet morning the Germans shelled Batt. H.Q. Offs which are situated about 1,000 yds down the main Communication Trench from the firing line to Bienvillers.	E/H

INTELLIGENCE SUMMARY
(Erase heading not required.)

Place	Date	Hour	Summary of Events and Information	Remarks and references to Appendices
Trenches	3.6.16	7pm	Altogether about a dozen shells landed very close to Bn. H.Q. dug-outs - doing however no damage - Size of shells 105mm	S/F
	4.6.16		Last night commencing at midnight our artillery heavily bombarded the enemy trenches opposite T92, T93 & T94. This was prior to a small trench raid made by the 10th Royal Fusiliers who are on our left. After ten minutes intense bombardment the enemy retaliated with 77mm, 105mm & 150mm shells, also a few minnenwerfer. Our left Coy sustained absolutely no casualties owing to the new 'slit' trenches recently dug by us. The left centre Company sustained 1 killed & 6 wounded, all the wounded were very slight. The whole shew seems	S/F

INTELLIGENCE SUMMARY

(Erase heading not required.)

Place	Date	Hour	Summary of Events and Information	Remarks and references to Appendices
Sucrie	4.6.16		was finished today by 2 A.m, and so far awhere been very quiet. The result of this raid made by the 10th R.F. Seems very same — as all they found was the remnants of German sentries blown to bits by our shells and 2 live farmers whom they bayonetted, bringing back no prisoners dead or alive.	S.H.
Sucrie 5 sept 16	5.6.16		Nil.	B.H. S.H.
	6.6.16		Very quiet night last night, nothing worth recording about	
Souly	7.6.16 10 a.m.		The 6th Leicester Regt. relieved this B. in trenches & we marched into billets at Souly.	S.B. E.O.
	8.6.16		Nil.	
	9.6.16		This morning the enemy bombarded L'Arbret - Souly Str. with 8" shells, 10 out of 30 being "blind".	O.K.

INTELLIGENCE SUMMARY.

(Erase heading not required.)

Place	Date	Hour	Summary of Events and Information	Remarks and references to Appendices
Sailly	9.6.16		Very little damage was done — only two trucks caught on fire, and the rails were churned up for about 100 yds from the Station.	S/t.
	10.6.16		Nil.	
	11.6.16		Two officers joined the Battalion — 2 Lieut Hayes from the 4th L N Lancs, and 2 Lieut S. Smith of the 20th Royal Fusiliers.	S/t. C/t D/t.
	12.6.16			
	13.6.16		Nil.	
	14.6.16		Nil.	
	15.6.16			
	16.6.16		Very large parties were called on to carry "Secret Stores" up to the front line. They had to march all the way from Sailly to Bienvillers; from thence they proceeded to the front line via hulke have to T 68 &c. These "Secret Stores" turned out to be Gas Cylinders.	S/t.

INTELLIGENCE SUMMARY

(Erase heading not required.)

Place	Date	Hour	Summary of Events and Information	Remarks and references to Appendices
Souly	17/6/16		The same (uniform coats or secret stores happened again) was carried out without a hitch.	S/L
"	18/6/16		Nil.	S/L
Bienvillers	19/6/16		The 1/6th N.L. train relieved the 6th Leicesters in support billets at Bienvillers. Relief was complete by 1.A.M. Lieut. C. G. Steel joined the Battalion from the 11th (Res.) K.N.L. Bn.	
	20.6.16 –22"		Nil.	
Trenches	23/6/16		The 1/6th Royal North Lancashire Rgt. relieved the 6th Bedfords in the trenches at 5·30 p.m., relief being complete at 7·15 p.m.	
"	24/6/16		This morning we heavily bombarded the enemies lines opposite Sommecourt – this bombardment lasted one day, at 4·30 p.m. firing ceased & our 'planes went up after which damage was observed. The enemy is in a bad & muddy condition.	S/L

INTELLIGENCE SUMMARY

(Erase heading not required.)

Place	Date	Hour	Summary of Events and Information	Remarks and references to Appendices
Trenches	25/6/16	10 a.m.	Enemy very active with minenwerfer & large shells. Heavy bombardment practically all day. Left on our immediate front & on the following points, ESSARTS, PIDGEON WOOD, la BRAYELLE FME, the "Z" and Gommecourt.	A+
"	26/6/16		Another severe bombardment by our Artillery evening replenish earlier than preceding day. Trenches still in a very bad condition, rained 2 or 3 times during the day.	
"	27/6/16		Reveille bombardment in the morning — at 2 p.m. we discharged some gas — the enemy few men reacted & retaliated with great vigor. Casualties up to date 4 & 6 O.Rs.	A+
"	28/6/16	10 a.m.	Gas was again repeated at 10.30 p.m. last night — never a retaliation rather feeble — Casualties Nil.	A+
"	29/6/16	10 a.m.	At 4 A.M. this morning the 7th & 6th Fusiliers B[?]s did a raid which was very successful.	A+

INTELLIGENCE SUMMARY.

and the Staff Manual respectively. Title pages will be prepared in manuscript.

(Erase heading not required.)

Place	Date	Hour	Summary of Events and Information	Remarks and references to Appendices
Trenches	30/6/16	10.30 p.m.	Last night the regiments on our right namely the 13th R. Bargd. & 13th K.R.Rs did one too raid. They brought in 2 prisoners, but the K.R.R.s lost 1 officer & 4 other ranks. This morning at dawn we opened a heavy bombardment on enemy trenches near Gommecourt, bu Bayelle etc. and at 9 AM a Smoke Cloud was sent over. Enemies retalliation extremely weak. To-night we are sending out a patrol of 1 officer & 26 o.ranks to raid the enemies trenches. They will be preceded by an intense T Mortar & Stokes guns bombardment.	St.
			Strength	
			Officers 33	
			Other ranks 858	
			Killed in action 16 o.Ranks	
			Wounded 2 Officers & 50 o.Ranks	
			Died of wounds Nil.	
			(1 man, S/Cpl Burns awarded the Green Card for gallantry.)	(See Major Milwain attd 1st or 3rd Dn' reinforcement depôt at Halloy & 2 Lieut. N Fisher to England for recruit training 29/6/16)

E. Howler
Lieut & Adjt
for OC 10th L N Lancs

112th Brigade.
37th Division
34th Division from 5.7.16

Transferred with 112th Brigade from
37th to 34th Division 5th July 1916.

1/10th BATTALION

LOYAL NORTH LANCASHIRE REGIMENT

JULY 1916

Army Form C. 2118.

WAR DIARY
or
INTELLIGENCE SUMMARY.
(Erase heading not required.)

Instructions regarding War Diaries and Intelligence Summaries are contained in F.S. Regs., Part II. and the Staff Manual respectively. Title pages will be prepared in manuscript.

Place	Date	Hour	Summary of Events and Information	Remarks and references to Appendices
Trenches	1/7/16		This morning at 7am 30 am we discharged smoke bombs & candles & did everything we could to attract the enemies attention while the 46th & 56th Divisions on our right attacked Gommecourt. The enemy retaliated pretty heavily we suffered only a few casualties.	P/C
"	2/7/16		The 4th Bde Rifles & Relieved us & we proceeded into support billets at Bienvillers – relief completed by 2.30 A.m. 3/7/16.	P/C
HALLOY	3/7/16		We marched by companies to Halloy – rest camp – here	S/C
"	4/7/16		We stayed. Bn Hd	S/C
"	5/7/16		Bn did usual sort of training when out of trenches. ditto	
MILLENCOURT	6/7/16		The Bn was moved from Halloy to Millencourt by 'Buses. The 111th & 112th Bde's were transferred from the 37th Div to 34th Div today. We now belong to 34th Division, III Corps, IV Army. The 110th Bde was transferred to 21st Division.	P/C
ALBERT	7/7/16		Today the Bn was taken up the Rue Vina Roches in ALBERT to be in support to the 23rd Division. We were not called upon.	P/C

WAR DIARY
or
INTELLIGENCE SUMMARY.
(Erase heading not required.)

Army Form C. 2118.

Instructions regarding War Diaries and Intelligence Summaries are contained in F. S. Regs., Part II. and the Staff Manual respectively. Title pages will be prepared in manuscript.

Place	Date	Hour	Summary of Events and Information	Remarks and references to Appendices
ALBERT	8/7/16		The Bn. is moved to Stand by ready to move at ½ an hours notice. After standing by all day we get orders to move at 8 p.m. to Tara Hill.	D/t.
Tara Hill	9/7/16		Nil	D/t.
"	10/7/16		Nil	D/t.
Trenches	11/7/16		To-day at 2 A.m. the Bn. relieved the 11th Warwicks in Trenches. The Enemy continually peppered us with gas shells & lachrimatory shells, which though disturbing did No damage.	D/t.
"	12/7/16		To-day the enemy being machine gunning we sustained many casualties including Capt. Dryden, Capt. Denney, Lieut. Bee, Lt. Atkinson, Lt. Smith 2nd Woolley.	D/t.
"	13/7/16		The Bn. was relieved by the 8th East Lancs, & we went into Close Support to them, at HELIGO LAND.	D/t.
"	14/7/16		Nil	D/o
"	15/7/16		Nil	D/o
"	16/7/16		The Bn. was ordered to proceed to the Chalk Pit in Close Support	2/t

WAR DIARY
or
INTELLIGENCE SUMMARY.
(Erase heading not required.)

Army Form C. 2118.

Place	Date	Hour	Summary of Events and Information	Remarks and references to Appendices
Trenches	16.7.16		to the 11th B'de who were to attack POZIERES. The attack commenced at 9 P.m. but they failed to gain their objective suffering very heavy casualties.	S/b
	17.7.16		At 4 P.m. the attack was renewed this B'n being the 4th wave of the attack, again however our objective was not reached as the whole village of POZIERES bristled with machine guns. We suffered about 40 casualties including Lieut Couper, Lieut Peskett, Lieut Hayes, Lieut Wren. Last night very late we relieved all the B'ns in the new advanced positions just outside Pozières and suffered nay 2 casualties in doing so doing.	S/b
	18.7.16		We were relieved by the 12th D.L.I. & proceeded into bivouacs in Tara Hill.	S/b
Tara Hill	19.7.16		Awaiting orders being in Reserve to the D.L.I's.	S/b
ALBERT	20.7.16 } 31.7.16		The B'n was relieved by the 11th B'n 1st B'de of the Australian Div.	S/b

WAR DIARY
or
INTELLIGENCE SUMMARY
(Erase heading not required.)

Army Form C. 2118

Instructions regarding War Diaries and Intelligence Summaries are contained in F.S. Regs., Part II. and the Staff Manual respectively. Title Pages will be prepared in manuscript.

Place	Date	Hour	Summary of Events and Information	Remarks and references to Appendices
ALBERT	21.7.16		& proceeded into billets at ALBERT.	Q.st.
LA HOUSSAYE	22.7.16		To-day at 8 A.M. the Bn moved to LA HOUSSAYE into rest billets.	Q.st.
"	23.7.16		The Bn is doing the usual training when out of trenches. 2nd Lieut. WOODWARD joined the Bn from the 11th (Res) Bn L.N. Lanc.	Q.st. / Q.tt.
"	24.7.16		2nd Lieut. Squibb awarded the Military Cross for good patrol work. 2nd Lieut. Waddow & 2nd Lieut. Pinches joined the Bn from the 3rd Bn Loyal North Lancs.	Q.st.
"	25.7.16		The 112th B'de was inspected by the Corps Comdr. (III Corps)	V.st.
"	26.7.16		Nil	Q.st.
"	27.7.16		} The Battalion practised the attack & although it was very	
"	28.7.16		} hot the recruits did very well	Q.st.
"	29.7.16		The B'de (112th) moved at 5 p.m. to BRESLE	Q.st.
BRESLE	30.7.16			
	31.7.16		The B'de marched from BRESLE to BECOURT WOOD, leaving Poole	Q.st.

Army Form C. 2118

WAR DIARY
or
INTELLIGENCE SUMMARY
(Erase heading not required.)

Instructions regarding War Diaries and Intelligence Summaries are contained in F. S. Regs., Part II. and the Staff Manual respectively. Title Pages will be prepared in manuscript.

Place	Date	Hour	Summary of Events and Information	Remarks and references to Appendices
BRESLE	31.7.16		at 6:30pm and arriving in Becourt Wood about 11 p.m.	S/d.
BECOURT WOOD	31.7.16	12 PM	Strength 31-7-16 Officers 18 o.Ranks 672 Officers killed Nil. Wounded Officers 11 o.Ranks 133 Rks 17 died of wounds officers 1 o.Ranks 6 missing 7 Drafts Officers — 3 o.Ranks — 9 $\overline{\frac{12}{1}}$ P.Howell Lieut & Adjutant for Lt-Colonel Comdg. 10th L.N. Lancs Rgt.	O.K.

112th Brigade.
34th Division till 22nd August
37th Division from 22nd August

1/10th BATTALION

THE LOYAL NORTH LANCASHIRE REGIMENT

AUGUST 1 9 1 6

Attached:-
Reports on Operations v 11th August 1916.

WAR DIARY
or
INTELLIGENCE SUMMARY

Army Form C. 2118

Place	Date	Hour	Summary of Events and Information	Remarks and references to Appendices
BECOURT WOOD	Aug 1st		The enemy shelling this wood very severely about 10 am this morning causing some 46 casualties in the 11th Berwicks B/ who are bivouacked on our left.	2/Lt.
"	2nd		To-day the 4 companies practised marching up & down trenches	
"	3.8.16		Ditto	2/Lt
"	4.8.16			2/Lt
"	5.8.16		To-day the Bn. relieved the 16th Bn. Royal Scots in MAMETZ WOOD.	2/Lt
Mametz Wood	6.8.16		The enemy fired several Gas Shells into the wood also manu B¼" & 9"	2/Lt
	7.8.16		Enemy's artillery very active — at least 50 shells of varying calibre — (4.2 & 5.9) were fired round Bn Hd qrs — we suffered 5 killed & 17 wounded	2/Lt

WAR DIARY

INTELLIGENCE SUMMARY

Army Form C. 2118

Place	Date	Hour	Summary of Events and Information	Remarks and references to Appendices
Mametz Wood	9/8/16		To-day the enemy has only shelled this wood intermittently during morning – we suffered no casualties.	
BAZENTIN-le-PETIT	10.8.16		This B[attalio]n relieved the 8th East Lancashire B[attalio]n in Trenches East of BAZENTIN-le-PETIT, the relief commencing at 4 p.m. & being complete by 6.30 p.m.	
BAZENTIN-le-PETIT 11.8.16			(At 2 A.m. this morning after 3 minutes bombardment 2 Companies – (A & C Coys) attacked a portion of trench called the intermediate Line. The line plan like this.	

MARTINPUICH →
N ↑
← BAZENTIN-le-PETIT
POZIERS

HIGH WOOD
ENGLISH
GERMAN Barricade
B.H.Qrs
"C" Coy

WAR DIARY
or
INTELLIGENCE SUMMARY

Army Form C. 2118

(Erase heading not required.)

Instructions regarding War Diaries and Intelligence Summaries are contained in F. S. Regs., Part II. and the Staff Manual respectively. Title Pages will be prepared in manuscript.

Place	Date	Hour	Summary of Events and Information	Remarks and references to Appendices
Mametz Wood	9/8/16		To-day the enemy has only shelled this wood intermittently during morning - we suffered no casualties. This Bn relieved the 8" East Lancashire Bn in Trenches East of BAZENTIN-le-PETIT, the relief commencing at 4 pm & being complete by 6.30pm.	
BAZENTIN -le- PETIT	10.8.16		At 2 AM. this morning 9/10 3 minute bombardment 2 Companies - (A & C Coys) attacked a portion of trench called the intermediate line. The line & plan like this.	

MARTINPUICH →
↑ N

POZIERES
HIGH WOOD
Bc.
ENGLISH
GERMAN Barricade
B.N. Hqrs

BAZENTIN-le-PETIT
BAZENTIN-le-GRAND

WAR DIARY
or
INTELLIGENCE SUMMARY

Army Form C. 2118

Place	Date	Hour	Summary of Events and Information	Remarks and references to Appendices
BAZENTIN le Petit	14/8/16		One Company (C) Commanded by Lieut. J.A. GRAVETT, (2nd in command 2/Lt WADESON) — As soon as the barrage lifted dashed along the top of the trench — throwing bombs as they went. The head of this company, being held up for a second, was ably supported by A Company under Lieut W.H. Procter (2nd in command 2/Lt A.F. GORDON) — This company charged along the top of the trench & jumped in — bayoneting & bombing all Germans within view. By 2.30 A.M. the trench as far as the road from BAZENTIN-le-Grand to MARTIN PUICH was entirely in our hands. Then 2/Lt Duggan with a party got together comprising men with picks & shovels & began to build a barricade about 50 yds from the road. This work was accomplished	

WAR DIARY
or
INTELLIGENCE SUMMARY
(Erase heading not required.)

Army Form C. 2118

Instructions regarding War Diaries and Intelligence Summaries are contained in F.S. Regs., Part II. and the Staff Manual respectively. Title Pages will be prepared in manuscript.

Place	Date	Hour	Summary of Events and Information	Remarks and references to Appendices
BAZENTIN le PETIT	11-9-16		by 2.50 AM — 2/Lt Duggan finding that Major all 4 officers were wounded (2/Lt Gordon - eventually dying) took command of the whole new line - length about 250 yds. At 3 AM. the enemy counterattack with great vim but were driven off by bombs & Lewis Guns. Again at 4 AM. the enemy counter attacked in force, but were driven off suffering very heavy Casualties. — a 3rd time at 5 AM. the enemy made a fresh attack & were once again driven off leaving many wounded. At 7 AM. the enemies artillery quieted & a new company (B Coy) were put in the trees line — A & C Companies being then withdrawn. The rest of the day passed quite quietly	

WAR DIARY or INTELLIGENCE SUMMARY

Army Form C. 2118

Place	Date	Hour	Summary of Events and Information	Remarks and references to Appendices
BAZENTIN le PETIT			The total casualties were Officers - Killed one, wounded 3. Other ranks Killed 20, wounded 77 = 97. Since died of wounds 7.	2 $
"	12-8-16		Day past quietly. At 10.30 p.m. last night the 11th Warwicks who are on our left attacked the intermediate line between the BAZENTIN-le-PETIT & BAZENTIN-le-GRAND roads after a heavy bombardment but failed to gain a footing, the M.Guns of the enemy being so concentrated.	
"	13-8-16		At 2.30 to-day the 15th Bn Royal Scots relieved us in trenches & we proceeded to BECOURT WOOD for the night.	
BRESLE	14-8-16		Bn. at 11 A.m. the Bn marched by Companies to BRESLE	2 $

WAR DIARY
or
INTELLIGENCE SUMMARY

(Erase heading not required.)

Army Form C. 2118

Instructions regarding War Diaries and Intelligence Summaries are contained in F.S. Regs., Part II. and the Staff Manual respectively. Title Pages will be prepared in manuscript.

Place	Date	Hour	Summary of Events and Information	Remarks and references to Appendices
LA HOUSSOYE	15/8/16		The Bn. oneneded from BRESLE - 16 LA HOUSSAYE at 2.30 p.m. arriving there at 5 p.m.	S/H
"	16/8/16		Nil	
"	17/8/16		Transport left by road for ALLONVILLE. Thence to LONGPRÉ.	S/H
				2/H
LONGPRÉ	18/8/16		The Bn. less (?) line transport entrained at FRECHENCOURT at 3 p.m. for LONGPRÉ arriving here at 10.30 p.m. The whole Bn. less transport billets.	S/H
"	19/8/16		Nil	2/H
Noeu Berquin	20/8/16		The Bn. entrained at Longpré Sta (including our transport) and proceeded to BAILLEUL, where they detrained and marched to Noeu BERQUIN, about 7 miles arriving at 8 A.M. Men rested all day at La Gorgue — good billets.	S/H (21+9/16)
	21/8/16			S/H
	22/8/16		The Bn. again entrained & proceeded to DIVION to rejoin 37 Division. The train left at 1.45 p.m. and arrived at DIVION at 5 p.m.	S/H

WAR DIARY
or
INTELLIGENCE SUMMARY
(Erase heading not required.)

Army Form C. 2118

Place	Date	Hour	Summary of Events and Information	Remarks and references to Appendices
BRUAY.	23/8/16		The Bn was billeted at Bruay, at 8pm, transport arriving at 12 MN.	Bn.
"	24.8.16	9am	The Bn has received orders to move to MAZINGARBE this afternoon and be attached to the 16th Division temporarily. IV Corps. I Army	Bn.
MAZINGARBE	24.8.16	6pm	The Bn marches here (Mazingarbe) into billets. Leaving BRUAY at 2pm. about 7 miles altogether. Officers were sent ahead to reconnoitre trenches which we will probably take over later.	Bn
MAZINGARBE	25.8.16		The Bn arrived here at 8pm last night. Orders first received to move to the North end of the village — men in huts at various billets. At completion of this move we come under the command of the G.O.C. 40th Division, 1st Corps, 1st Army. Our Brigade dispositions are as follows.	Bn.
			8th EAST Lancs in line. (on the right:) 6th Bedfords " " (on the left:) 11th Warwicks : Support 10th L N Lancs : Reserve.	S.A.

WAR DIARY
or
INTELLIGENCE SUMMARY
(Erase heading not required.)

Army Form C. 2118

Instructions regarding War Diaries and Intelligence Summaries are contained in F. S. Regs., Part II. and the Staff Manual respectively. Title Pages will be prepared in manuscript.

Place	Date	Hour	Summary of Events and Information	Remarks and references to Appendices
MAZINGARBE	26.8.16		The Bn had to furnish "Caretakers" for various redoubts in the 2nd line defences. Caretakers consisted of about 1 N.C.O. & 4 men average. The evening we had to supply a working party of 150 o.Ranks.	Sgt.
"	27.8.16		Nil.	Dr
"	28.8.16		Nil.	E.Lt
TRENCHES	29.8.16		The Bn relieved the 6th Badgers in the 14 Bis Sector — that is between HULLUCH & LOOS. The relief was carried out well & all was complete by the 6 p.m. On account of almost torrential rain no work was done in the trenches. Enemy very quiet.	Sgt.
	30.8.16		Enemy very quiet — weather still bad	Dr
	31.8.16		The Bn is being relieved tomorrow the 1st of September 1916.	
MAZINGARBE				

E. Howell
Lieut & adjt
for O.C. 10th Bn Loyal N. Lancs V.V.

10th Loyal North Lancs

Original Reports
on Operations
11th August 1916

B.G.C. 112th Brigade   5-25 a.m.
                            13 Aug.

I beg to report as follows:-

To assist the 11th R Warwicks my Batt? fired 40 Rifle Grenades into the German Trench over & about the road in S 2 D up to 10-33 P.M.

At 10.33 P.M. 2/Lt ROSTRON & a party of Bombers rushed towards the road to assist the Warwicks by diverting the enemy's attention. They succeeded in getting close up to the road when a machine gun opened fire from the W. of the road at close range.

His party attacked it with bombs but failed to dislodge it — He saw & heard no signs of the Warwicks.

He then returned & got more bombs & advanced again, this time in the trench past our new barricade & succeeded in again getting close up to the road, here he proceeded to construct a new barricade, whilst consolidating this, heavy machine gun fire in enfilade was opened on him from the West & a large number of Germans, who had crawled up in shell holes, bombed him heavily.

He therefore ~~retired~~ withdrew behind our barricade bringing in our wounded — Our losses are some 15 men wounded bombs & M.G. bullets.

R. Cobbold
Lt Colonel
Comdg 10th L.N. Lancs.

B.G.C. 112th Brigade.
6.30 am Aug 11th

I beg to forward herewith a preliminary account of the operation against the Intermediate line which my Battalion undertook early this morning.

The Objective was that part of the Intermediate line from the Barricade at about S 2 D 9 6 to the road Westwards where it crosses the Intermediate line.

In order to avoid as far as possible the Enemy barrage I determined to attack en enfilade in preference to a frontal attack.

The Dispositions were that two Companies were employed. I withdrew from the remaining 2 Cos all their best Bombers & mixed them with the fighting groups of the Cos. detailed for the attack.

Lt. GRAVETT "C" Coy. was detailed to lead the attack with 'A' Coy. Lt. PROCTOR in support.

2

These 2 Cos occupied the line previous to the attack "C" on the left "A" on the right their place being taken by the Coy. in close Support as they formed their dispositions previous to Zero time.

A ramp was constructed to enable the men to get out of the trench quickly & by 1.55 a.m. — (Zero being 2 a.m.) the leading Coy. were all above ground in proper formation.

I ordered the O.C. "A" Coy. to sweep the objective & either side of it thoroughly with Lewis Gun Fire from 1.55 a.m till 2-2 a.m. & stationed 4 Rifle Grenade men on the top near the barricade to continue firing rifle grenades over the attacking Infantry into the trench & along each side of it.

Lt. GRAVETT led the attack with 20 Bombers carrying waistcoats 10 bombs in each — each man with rifle bayonet fixed, slung.

3

Behind him 4 fighting groups under their own N.C.O's with whom they have rec'd. instructions - 9 men in each group - bombers wearing waistcoats 10 bombs each - Every man, in addition, carried two bombs each. Behind these trench clearers and men carrying buckets of bombs. (all these in the trench) - The L.G. were on the right flank, one fired ahead, the second swept the ground to the North, ie the right flank

A right flank guard 50 yards from the trench was to sweep up snipers

As soon as the last men of "C" Coy passed the Barricade the orders were for the leading group of "A" Coy to get into the trench & follow on - the 2 last groups to carry 1 pick & 1 shovel each - 2 groups carrying buckets of bombs.

In addition one selected N.C.O & 12

4

Expert bombers & determined men were selected to advance along the left, or S side of the trench – in order to support "C" Coy. if held up, & take the enemy in rear.

The Artillery Barrage is reported to have been weak & ineffective, in fact the Officers inform me that they could not have told when the barrage lifted at Zero, had they not been accurately clocked. It did not keep the enemy snipers heads down nor apparently interfere with their M.G. fire.

At Zero precisely Lt GRAVETT leading his 20 Bombers rushed along the trench as they passed the Barricade, throwing bombs into the trench & passing on at the Double. The remaining groups followed on, some in the trench some outside, as detailed. There was little opposition for 100 yards, when

5

The enemy began to throw bombs from the trench & put up the S.O.S signal & many flares. The men took cover in shell holes & crept forward throwing bombs the groups doing their work in the trench. At about 150 yds the enemy opened machine gun fire with 2 MG's from the road & enfiladed the trench & both sides & under a shower of bombs our men fell back there being many casualties. Lt. Gravett was here wounded by shrapnel & incapacitated from throwing bombs. - Lt. Proctor & party now came up on the left side of the trench & attacked the Bosche vigorously, driving them back & carrying the whole attack on again.

The men shouted out "BOLTON" - "BOLTON" - being apparently mostly men from that town

6

& they charged forward in the trench some men still under L̲t̲ GRAVETT still on top & bombing & finally drove the enemy back over the road. The last 40 yards being quite straight & a M.G. firing from behind the road dead into the trench — after several men had been knocked out — it was decided to block the trench at this point — which was done — & a second barricade erected 40 yards further back. The first barricade being held & L.G's in position.

The enemy fired great numbers of rifle grenades as the attackers advanced into the trench & on either side. L̲t̲ GRAVETT was a second time wounded in the head by a bomb, but remained most gallantly

7

in command of his men till the trench was finally taken & consolidated — Lt Proctor was also wounded in two places by bullet & bomb. These were the only two officers concerned in the actual attack & are the only officers in the Companies which took part in the operation.

The enemy bombarded the captured trench heavily at once & continuously & the officer who was placed on guard at the new barricade has just been severely wounded. This leaves me actually with 4 – 2nd Lieutenants – myself, my second in Command, & my Adjutant.

8

Inless men have suffered heavily & altho' I have not yet received the total list of casualties. I fear that the two Companies concerned have lost 50 per cent in killed & wounded. Both the Company Serjt. Majors were killed. I am informed by the Medical Officer & by my Second in Command that the men are however in good spirits & have got unlimited pluck in them notwithstanding.

At 5.45 am the enemy made a determined counter attack. Crossing the road & attacking our barricade in the trench whilst large numbers attacked across the open from another trench near the road

9

These attacks were all beaten off & the enemy driven back over the road - The L G's killed a considerable number in the open -

In the Trench itself 20 Germans were killed - The remainder scattered across the open & across the road - The L G's doing good execution -

I cannot speak too highly of the gallantry & determination of Lt. Proctor & Lt GRAVETT. who personally led their men with very great courage & I wish to recommend these

16

Officers for the Military Cross
- Lt Proctors jaw is Smashed.
Lt GRAVETT I trust is not
so severely wounded.

I will send you later on
a fuller account of the
operation as soon as I
receive all details.

R. Cobbold
Lt. Colonel
Comdg 10th Loyal N. Lancs

B.G.C. 112th Brigade

Following on my previous report
The casualties so far as I can
gather amount to about
    113 — I cannot say how
many of these are killed.
In addition 2/Lt. GORDON who
joined last week is killed —

The trench was full of Germans
who fought most determinedly —
They were driven back to the road
& over it, and our men went
on to the road — but as the last
40 yards E of the road is straight
& very much damaged — in fact

2

it is flat & no trench exists — there was obviously no reason to hold it. A sandbag barricade has been erected 40 yds from the road — then barbed wire across the trench — & then another barricade of Sandbags. Close to the road within 100 x of it the trench is much damaged by our fire & very shallow in places —

The trench is being deepened & slits dug for protection from Enfilade fire.

The enemy counter attacked from direction of the Trench & across the open (from left Flank) at 3.15 4.30 am & 5 am. The first two attacks being pressed right up to the trench. Three Lewis

3

Guns were in position & a great number of the enemy were killed.

There was a great deal of difficulty with the L.G. Ammunition, in Discs, ran short, dirt got in the Discs, jams occurred, most of the teams were new men, but they accounted for a lot of Bosche.

The counter attacks appeared to come from another bit of Trench just East of the road & about 200 yards North of the Intermediate trench.

The enemy snipers were scattered in Shell holes. The right flanking party did good work clearing them. Lt. GRAVETT shot several

4

with his revolver —

There is one shaft in the trench taken.

A new bomb or Rifle grenade thrower was captured with a book of directions —

We suffered a few casualties from our own shell fire —

The enemy machine guns were numerous mostly from direction N.W. by N.

The .77 mm barrage put down by the enemy came from High Wood Direction.

My Platoon in close support had 21 casualties.

Aug 11th

R. Cobbold Lt. Col.
Comdg 10th Loyal N. Lancs

B.G.C., 112th Brigade.　　　　　　6.30 am Aug. 11th.

　　　I beg to forward herewith a preliminary account of the operations against the Intermediate Line which my Battalion undertook early this morning.

　　　My objective was that part of the Intermediate Line from the Barricade at about S.2.d.9.6. to the road Westwards where it crosses the Intermediate Line.

　　　In order to avoid as far as possible the enemy barrage I determined to attack en enfilade in preference to a frontal attack.

　　　The dispositions were that two Companies were employed. I withdrew from the remaining 2 Co's all their best bombers and mixed them with the fighting groups of the Co's detailed for the attack.

　　　Lt. GRAVETT "C" Coy. was detailed to lead the attack with "A" Coy. Lt. PROCTOR in support.

　　　These two Co's occupied the line previous to the attack "C" on the left "A" on the right, their place being taken by the Coy. in close support as they formed their dispositions previous to zero time.

　　　A ramp was constructed to enable the men to get out of the trench quickly & by 1.55 am (zero being 2 am) the leading Coy. were all above ground in proper formation.

　　　I ordered the O.C. "A" Coy. to sweep the objective and either side of it thoroughly with Lewis Gun fire from 1.55 am till 2.2 am and stationed 4 Rifle Grenade men on the top near the barricade to continue firing rifle grenades over the attacking infantry into the trench and along each side of it.

　　　Lt. GRAVETT led the attack with 30 bombers carrying waistcoats, 10 bombs in each, each man with rifle bayonet fixed slung.

　　　Behind him 4 fighting groups under their own N.C.O's with whom they have recd. instruction - 9 men in each group - bombers wearing waistcoats, 10 bombs each - every man, in addition, carried 2 bombs each. Behind these trench clearers and men carrying buckets of bombs (all these in the trench).

　　　The L.G. were on the right flank, one fired ahead, the second swept the ground to the North, i.e. the right flank.

　　　A right flank guard 50 yards from the trench was to sweep up snipers.

　　　As soon as the last men of "C" Coy. passed the Barricade the orders were for the leading group of "A" Coy. to get into the trench and follow on - the 2 last groups to carry 1 pick and 1 shovel each - 2 groups carrying buckets of bombs.

In addition 1 selected N.C.O. and 12 expert bombers and determined men were selected to advance along the left or S. side of the trench, in order to support "C" Coy. if held up and take the enemy in rear.

The artillery barrage is reported to have been weak and in effective, in fact the officers inform me that they could not have told when the barrage lifted at zero had they not been accurately clocked. It did not keep the enemy's snipers' heads down nor apparently interfere with their M.G. fire.

At zero precisely Lt. GRAVETT leading his 20 bombers rushed along the trench as they passed the barricade, throwing bombs into the trench and passing on at the double. The remaining groups followed on, some in the trench, some outside, as detailed. There was little opposition for 100 yards, when the enemy began to throw bombs from the trench and put up the S.O.S. signal and many flares. The men took cover in shell holes and crept forward throwing bombs, the groups doing their work in the trench. At about 150 yards the enemy opened machine gun fire with 2 M.G's from the road and enfiladed the trench and both sides and under a shower of bombs our men fell back there being many casualties. Lt. GRAVETT was here wounded by shrapnel and incapacitated from throwing bombs.

Lt. PROCTOR and party now came up on the left side of the trench and attacked the Bosche vigprpusly, driving them back and carrying the whole attack on again.

The men shouted out "BOLTON "BOLTON" being apparently meatly men from that town and they charged forward in the trench some men still under Lt. GRAVETT still on top and bombing and finalyy drove the enemy back over the road. The last 40 yards being quite straight and a M.G. firing from behind the road dead into the trench, after several men had been knocked out it was decided to block the trench at this point, which was done and a second barricade erected 40 yards further back. The first barricade being held & L.G's in position.

The enemy fired great numbers of rifle grenades as the attackers advanced into the trench and on either side. Lt. GRAVETT was a $second time wounded in the head by a bomb but remained most gallantly in command of his men till the trench was finally taken and consolidated. Lt. PROCTOR was also wounded in two places by bullet and bomb. These were the only two officers concerned in the actual attack and are the only officers in the Companies which took part in the operation.

The enemy bombarded the captured trench heavily at once and continuously and the officer who was placed on guard at the new barricade has just been severely wounded.

At 4.45 am the enemy made a determined counter-attack, crossing the road and attacking our barricade

3.

in the trench whilst large numbers attacked across the open from another trench near the road. These attacks were all beaten off and the enemy driven back over the road. The L.G's killed a considerable number in the open.

In the trench itself 20 Germans were killed. The remainder scattered across the open and across the road, the L.G's doing good execution.

I cannot speak too highly of the gallantry and determination of Lt. PROCTOR and Lt. GRAVETT who personally led their men with very great courage and I wish to recommend these Officers for the Military Cross. Lt. PROCTOR's jaw is smashed. Lt. GRAVETT I trust is not so severely wounded.

                                    (sd) R.Cobbold, Lt-Colonel.
                                    Comdg. 10th Loyal N.Lancs.

112th Brigade.
37th Division.

1/10th BATTALION

LOYAL NORTH LANCASHIRE REGIMENT

SEPTEMBER 1 9 1 6

INTELLIGENCE SUMMARY

Instructions regarding War Diaries and Intelligence Summaries are contained in F.S. Regs., Part II. and the Staff Manual respectively. Title Pages will be prepared in manuscript.

(Erase heading not required.)

Place	Date	Hour	Summary of Events and Information	Remarks and references to Appendices
MAZINGARBE	1-9-16	10 p.m.	The Bn. was relieved in trenches by the 6th Bn. King's Own Liverpools Regt. 76th Bde., III Division – & proceeded into billets at Mazingarbe.	BH.
BEUGIN	2.9.16		The Batt'n marched to BEUGIN (DIÉVAL area) leaving Mazingarbe at 1.30 p.m. and arriving at Beugin at 7.50 p.m. The men's feet were in bad marching order consequently men to men fell out on the way. 2/hour workout is The billets are good though a little cramped. appointed Town Major temporarily of Beugin.	BH.
–do–	3.9.16		Companies took the men to bathe in a lake close to billets. Kits inspected & differences made up.	BH.
–do–	4.9.16		2/Lieuts Bennett, Baird, Travers & Beastall joined from the 14th Sherwood Foresters.	BH.
–do–	5.9.16		The G.O.C. 37th Division inspected the Battn. and seemed well pleased with the Battn. Sgt Wood, Cpl Gregg, Ptes Johnson, Taylor, Longworth & Machinnon, & L/Cpl Sadden C.S.M. Richardson being awarded M.M.'s & Honours at the 11th Btn.	BH.

INTELLIGENCE SUMMARY

(Erase heading not required.)

Place	Date	Hour	Summary of Events and Information	Remarks and references to Appendices
Bengin	6/9/16		Companies continued training in men in bombing, Lewis guns etc.	S.
"	7/9/16		NIL	P.H.
"	8.9.16		Sjeut Proctor awarded the DSO L/Craovert & 21St Bugger to Military Cross. Pte Rickings to Pelu Pte Scwingers the M.M.	S.H.
"	9.9.16		NIL	P.H.
"	10.9.16		B'de (112) held a horse show — half holiday for the men.	P.H.
"	11.9.16		Swimming gala held close to Battn billets.	P.H.
"	12.9.16		NIL	P.H.
"	13.9.16		Officers & 50 men were detailed to Brana digging fatigue to Curigny farm. The dispositions which is Reserve are, Bengin 10th L.N.L. BEUGIN — 11th Warwicks at La Comté, 6" Bayons & 8"East Lanes, M.G. Coy & 112" T.M.B. at Diéval. B'de H.Qrs. at Château Seaudure. B.G.C. 112" B'de held a conference of all C.O's, adjts & Coy Comdts to discuss points of interest during the recent fighting on the Somme.	P.H.
"	14/9/16		LEAVE appears to resume the 15th inst —	D.H.
Beugin	15/9/16		Lieut Boronye and 2/Lt Allen and an N.C.O proceeded on leave to Ryland until the 24th inst.	D.H.

INTELLIGENCE SUMMARY

Instructions regarding War Diaries and Intelligence Summaries are contained in F.S. Regs., Part II and the Staff Manual respectively. Title Pages will be prepared in manuscript.

(Erase heading not required.)

Place	Date	Hour	Summary of Events and Information	Remarks and references to Appendices
BEUGIN	16/9/16		NIL.	
"	17.9.16		Orders received to move into the forward area – Advance Section to-morrow. The 18th Commanding officers went to Paris for 2 days leave at 8. a.m. the Batty proceeded from Beugin, via Houdain, Bruay	S.A.
HERSIN	18.9.16		etc. to HERSIN – where we stayed the night.	S.A.
FOSSE 10	19.9.16		The Batty. resumed the march to FOSSE 10, one and a half miles from Hersin and 1 mile from Bully Grenay. We relieved the 1st Royal Marine Light Infantry, 188th Bde 63rd Division. Our dispositions were follows, Battalion H.Qrs. with 2 Coys remained at FOSSE 10, the other two companies went to Bully Grenay – the Battn. is in reserve. The remainder of the Brigade is situated thus 1st Warwicks in support – with H.Qts & 2 Coys in Bully Grenay and 2 Coys in Reserve Trenches 6th Bedford & 8th Easterns in front line 12th B de H.Qs. our Left. Our Bully Grenay. 63rd Inf Bde on our right and 111th Inf Bde on our left.	S.A.

INTELLIGENCE SUMMARY

(Erase heading not required.)

Summaries are contained in F. S. Regs., Part II. and the Staff Manual respectively. Title Pages will be prepared in manuscript.

Place	Date	Hour	Summary of Events and Information	Remarks and references to Appendices
Fosse 10	21.9.16	20/9/16	Nil.	
"	22.9.16		The C.O. arrived back from leave. 2/Lieut H.T.G. Duggan promoted Lieut. vide London Gazette Sept 20th. 2/Lieut E.H. PINCHES and 2/Lieut E.T. WADESON (on post) confirmed in their rank – Sept 20th 1916	SA
"	23.9.16		Nil.	
"	24.9.16		Nil.	
Yincker	25.9.16		To-day at 8AM this Battn. relieved the 6th Beafords in the line. Relief complete by 11.30am.	SA
"	26.9.16		Very quiet day – Dispositions as follows, "B" Coy on the right of the front line "C" Coy on left. A Company in support, "D" Company in reserve. The right companies H.Q'rs are subject to much minenwerfer fire. Considerable T.Mortar activity on both sides – No damage done by the enemy in our trenches.	SA

INTELLIGENCE SUMMARY

(Erase heading not required.)

Place	Date	Hour	Summary of Events and Information	Remarks and references to Appendices
TRENCHES	27/9/16		Last night the enemy "minenwerfered" our right Company pretty severely – the Support Battery (A/126) was called upon to give assistance & eventually silenced the enemy. 2/Lieut Roshin took a small patrol out to examine then an old disused trench; last night the trench ran something like this:	
			GERMAN TRENCHES / DISUSED TRENCHES / BRITISH LINE	
"	28/9/16		This trench showed signs of recent occupation – but nothing of interest was found	
"	29/9/16		To-day the enemy were very aggressive with "minenwerfer" but we called artillery and silenced them. 2/Lieut Roshin & 2 men examined the sunken road leading from X ---- to X	

INTELLIGENCE SUMMARY

(Erase heading not required.)

Summaries are contained in F. S. Regs., Part II. and the Staff Manual respectively. Title Pages will be prepared in manuscript.

Place	Date	Hour	Summary of Events and Information	Remarks and references to Appendices
Treuten	30.9.16		Very quiet day. The 6th Bedfords relieved us to-morrow. Casualties during the tour 1 man. LIEUTENANT & acting ADJUTANT. E. HOWELL appointed ADJT. from 16-5-16. D Stanley Lieut & adjt for O.C. 10th L.N. Lancs.	O/R

112th Brigade.
37th Division.

1/10th LOYAL NORTH LANCASHIRE REGIMENT

OCTOBER 1916

INTELLIGENCE SUMMARY

'Summaries are contained in F.S. Regs., Part II. and the Staff Manual respectively. Title Pages will be prepared in manuscript.'

(Erase heading not required.)

Place	Date	Hour	Summary of Events and Information	Remarks and references to Appendices
BULLY-GRENAY	1.10.16		The Battn. was relieved this morning by 6th Bedfords & proceeded to the Support Village – Bully-Grenay. Disposition are: 1 Company, Close Support – Meinicke line ½ a Company in Cap-de-Port Trenches: ½ a Company in the Village of Grenos D'Aix – remainder of Battn. i.e. 2 Companies & H.Qrs. at BULLY-GRENAY.	Btt.
"	2.10.16		The Exhausting Officer went on leave this morning for 10 days. 90 men arrived as a draft. Goodserf men use fired 350 men each day for working parties	Btt.
"	3.10.16		The B.G.C. held a conference at H.Qrs. 112 Bde. for Commanding officers to explain about itinerus maneouvres etc.	Btt.
"	4.10.16		NIL.	Btt.
"	5.10.16		NIL.	Btt.
"	6.10.16		Le-Quesnoy. We go to relieve 6th Bedgers in Trenches Major R Litinguet – 6th Bedgers assumes command of this Battn.	Btt.
Trenches	7.10.16			Btt.

INTELLIGENCE SUMMARY

(Erase heading not required.)

Summaries are contained in F. S. Regs., Part II and the Staff Manual respectively. Title Pages will be prepared in manuscript.

Place	Date	Hour	Summary of Events and Information	Remarks and references to Appendices
Trenches	7.10.16		Relieve commenced at 9am & was completed by 10am. 21st Bn with accidentally wounded himself with a rifle Reveille.	S/R
"	8.10.16		We were heavily Trininewefers this morning, 2/Lt Peters wounded the enemy resulted otherwise.	S/R
"	9.10.16		To-day the Bn. ~~got~~ was relieved of one Company frontage by the 63" Bde and took over one Co frontage from the 11" Warwicks on my left. My line has now run from SOP 15 I believe to Bully Alley trench inclusive. One man killed to-day 9ft & two others wounded by trininewefer.	
"	10/10/16 11/10/16		Nil.	R/R
"	12.10.16		Enemy very Quiet.	R/R
Fosse 10	13.10.16		We were relieved by the 6 Beds. this turning, the CO returns from leave	R/R
"	14.10.16		Nil	

INTELLIGENCE SUMMARY

Summaries are contained in F. S. Regs., Part II. and the Staff Manual respectively. Title Pages will be prepared in manuscript.

(Erase heading not required.)

Place	Date	Hour	Summary of Events and Information.	Remarks and references to Appendices
FOSSE 10/ HERMIN	15/10/16		To-day the 28th French Canadian Bn relieved us and we marched to HERMIN about 8 miles from Fosse 10.	S.M.
DIÉVAL	16.10.16		Battalion had a kit inspection. A draft of 75 other ranks arrived. Very sudden widespread men.	B.O.
"	17.10.16		Nil.	B.O.
AVERDOINGT	18.10.16		The Battalion marched from Dieval leaving there at 8.30 a.m. arriving at Averdoingt at 1 p.m.	B.O.
"	19.10.16		The Companies reorganises the new draft. Cleaning up generally.	B.O.
SÉRICOURT	20.10.16		The Battn continued its march to SÉRICOURT — 2½ kilometres from French Billets were dirty & very cramped.	B.O.
HEM	21/10/16		This morning at 7.15 a.m. the Bn continued the march from	S.O.

INTELLIGENCE SUMMARY

summaries are contained in F.S. Regs., Part II.
and the Staff Manual respectively. Title Pages
will be prepared in manuscript.

(Erase heading not required.)

Place	Date	Hour	Summary of Events and Information	Remarks and references to Appendixes
HEM	21.10.16		Sericourt 15 HEM — 1 mile west of DOULLENS. Packs were carried by motor lorry – men marched – distance about 10 miles. This – the 34th Division is now in the 5th Corps, Reserve Army.	
Mericourt	22.10.16		To-day the Bn. marched from Hem to Mericourt about 6 miles S. East of Doullens. Very cramped in billets. &c	
Beausart	23.10.16		Bn. again marched this morning to Beausart leaving Mericourt at 9am. – march was about 8 miles, roads here are very bad. The C.O. & the Adjutant went by lurry to see the communication trenches. An attack is impending.	
"	24/10/16		The Bde (112) is attached to the 2nd Division, & is supporting the 99. Bde. The weather hitherto in his area & tents very bad.	&c

INTELLIGENCE SUMMARY

(Erase heading not required.)

Place	Date	Hour	Summary of Events and Information	Remarks and references to Appendices
VAUCHELLES	25/10/16		To-day the Battn marched to Vauchelles in the week area – about 8½ miles – left Beauvoir at 9.30 a.m. arriving here at 12.30 p.m.	S/L
"	26/10/16		Men are all in good billets – officers billets are bad.	S/L
"	27/10/16		Moved training when every Trenches – carried on. To-day the Bn practised the attack. Weather unfavourable.	Op/L
"	28/10/16		2 men were accidentally bayoneted. 2/Lr Macnamara rejoined the Bn from England, & reported to 'A' Coy.	S/L
"	29/10/16		Nil	S/L
Amplier	30/10/16		To-day the Bn marched from Vauchelles – en route to GEZAINCOURT – when we were ¾ of the way there our billeting area was changed to the Bn had to march back 2 miles to Amplier & Amplier. There are no billets here & officers & men had to sleep in very bad huts.	S/L

INTELLIGENCE SUMMARY

(Erase heading not required.)

Place	Date	Hour	Summary of Events and Information	Remarks and references to Appendices
POULLE[N]S	3/10/16		This morning the Bn marched from Pouillens about 3 miles:- Officers & men have good billets. 2/Lieuts Vipond, Vernon & Tong joined the Bn. 1st Bn Royce Withers Capt. Chew of the 15th North Staffs joined the Bn is appointed OC "C" Coy. Ampliers to Bn from the Blt.	Hanru Lieut Regt for OC 18t L.N. Lancs

112th Brigade.
37th Division.

1/10th LOYAL NORTH LANCASHIRE REGIMENT

NOVEMBER 1916

Appendices attached:-

Attack on MUNICH TRENCH

WAR DIARY
or
INTELLIGENCE SUMMARY
(Erase heading not required.)

Place	Date	Hour	Summary of Events and Information	Remarks and references to Appendices
Doullens	1/11/16		Thorough kit inspection for whole Bn. Steps taken to replace from the Bn. base anything lost by men.	B/r
"	2/11/16		Bn. Parade under Company Arrangements.	B/r
"	3/11/16		2/Lt. Tongo sent to Hospital – Draft of 46 other ranks arrived. The B'dr had a practise attack – 10-day commencing at 9am. & finishing about 11.30am.	B/r
"	4/11/16		The B'dr had another practise attack over the same country – the Batts. got back into billets at 1.30pm.	B/r
"	5/11/16		Parades under Coy arrangements. A. & Q.C.M. was held in Pte Crawford for being drunk and striking a Superior officer. – Sentence 90 days F.P. No I.	S/b
"	6/11/16		Parades – Batts.	P/b
"	7/11/16		10-day Coy made their own arrangements about parades	S.B.
"	8/11/16		this morning we had a terrible bombing accident in which 2/Lt. Traver, 2/Lt. Vernon were killed, 2/Lt. Stacey wounded, Sgt. Milton severely wounded, Ptes Smith & Hamer wounded	S/B

WAR DIARY
INTELLIGENCE SUMMARY
(Erase heading not required.)

Army Form C. 2118

Instructions regarding War Diaries and Intelligence Summaries are contained in F.S. Regs., Part II. and the Staff Manual respectively. Title Pages will be prepared in manuscript.

Place	Date	Hour	Summary of Events and Information	Remarks and references to Appendices
Doullens	8/11/16		The cause of the accident was apparently the premature burst of a Mills No 1 Grenade which was thrown by 2/Lt Vernon. Count Enguym was held the verdict being that No one present was to blame.	8/t
"	9/11/16		At 2.30 pm to-day the funeral of the late 2/Lt's Travers & Vernon took place, they were buried in the civilian Cemetery, Doullens.	9/t
"	10/11/16		To-day Cos. carried on usual programme of work. 2/Lt Walmesley joined the Bn from the 1/4th Royal W. Kent Regt.	S/t
"	11/11/16		The B.G.C. inspected the billets & found everything in order.	8/t
Vauchelles	12/11/16		This morning the Bn left Doullens at 12.30 p.m. & marched direct here (Vauchelles). Billets very cramped. "Z" day has been fixed for to-morrow — We are in Corps reserve	
BERTRANCOURT	13/11/16	6 pm	To-day being 'Z' day we moved up to BERTRANCOURT & are now under the G.O.C. 3rd Division. So far the attack all along	9/t

WAR DIARY
or
INTELLIGENCE SUMMARY

(Erase heading not required.)

Instructions regarding War Diaries and Intelligence Summaries are contained in F.S. Regs., Part II. and the Staff Manual respectively. Title Pages will be prepared in manuscript.

Place	Date	Hour	Summary of Events and Information	Remarks and references to Appendices
BERTRAN-COURT	13/11/16	10 pm	the line has been most successful & kept at SERRE — & which piece the 3rd Division has been held up.	S/r.
MAILLY-MAILLET	14/11/16	5 pm	This morning the Batt. marched from Betrancourt to Mailly — of which piece came under the command of the G.O. of 2nd Division	S/10.
"	14/11/16 10.15 p.		Orders have just been received for the 5th M. Bde. (also the 8th Scot Lanc) to go & relieve the 5th M. Bde. & ultimately to relieve the 16th Bedfs & 11th Warwks which lost regts did an attack this afternoon. At present the enemy are shelling the village — so far no damage.	2/r.
	15/11/16		This morning saw the Batt. been ordered up to the front line trenches. At 8.30 a.m. the B. was formed up in artillery formation and with the 51st Division on the right, and the 8th Division on the left we advanced to — main a German line known as the Munich Trench — our own barrage was intense but very inaccurate — causing a great many casualties.	S/t

Summaries are contained in F.S. Regs., Part II.
and the Staff Manual respectively. Title Pages
will be prepared in manuscript.

INTELLIGENCE SUMMARY

(Erase heading not required.)

Place	Date	Hour	Summary of Events and Information	Remarks and references to Appendices
Original German 3rd line trenches	15/11		By 1 p.m. to-day – reports came in that we had failed to gain a footing in Munich Trench – our own barrage having killed & wounded so many of our men. Amongst those killed were Capt. Chew, Lieut. Cooper, Reid, Tudor. 2/Lt. Bennett, 2/Lt. Slavin, and 2/Lieut Andrew. Officers wounded were, 2/Lieuts Knauft, Beadle, Bradbury, Baird, Macnamara. ✗ This Officer eventually succeeded to his wounds. Our very quiet except for sudden barrages by the enemy coming over the guns. There is terrible congestion of wounded. The IV Division relieved us this afternoon in our advanced positions and we retired to the original German 2nd line. (Q.S.a.5.o to Q.S.a.5.8.)	D/S. D/S.
"	16/11/16	8am	This morning at 8 am to Bonny St. relieved us & we retired to Mailly Maillet arriving here at 6 a.m. There we are awfully dirty. This afternoon at 2 pm we marched to Puchevillers	D/S.
Mailly–Maillet – Puchevillers	"	6pm		
"	"	10pm	all arrived very happily. Orders just received to move to – move to Naours.	20

INTELLIGENCE SUMMARY

(Erase heading not required.)

Instructions regarding War Diaries and Intelligence Summaries are contained in F.S. Regs., Part II. and the Staff Manual respectively. Title Pages will be prepared in manuscript.

Place	Date	Hour	Summary of Events and Information	Remarks and references to Appendices
Station R^d between BEAUMONT-HAMEL and BEAUCOURT	18/11/16	1am	This morning we left ENGLEBELMER at 7.30 a.m. and rested for two hours in the British original front line trenches just East of HAMEL. At 12 noon we turned in here to Station Road — this is a Sunken Road in a valley — it runs from BEAUCOURT to Beaumont-Hamel. Here we are in support to the 6th Bedford. Sh.	
- do -	19/11/16		This Battⁿ came up rations to the 6th Bedford.	8/6
"	20/11/16	4pm	At 4pm. to-day a shell burst in to midst of several officers in in was killed instantly. Those received are Major Milvair, Captⁿ Donovan (Raine) 2Lt^s Woodward and Renshall. Gunn wounded. 2Lts Allen & Lieut Walton. Shook & stunned. Shook and 4 other rank wounded. N.K.	9/Y 8/6
"	21/11/16		We relieve the 6th Bedford at 5pm this evening	9/Y 8/6
"	22/11/16		During relief last night we had 2 killed & 4 other ranks wounded. Trenches are in a different state.	
Trenches	23/11/16	4.30pm	At 4:30pm this afternoon we are to attack a triangle position in rather like this	

INTELLIGENCE SUMMARY

(Erase heading not required.)

Instructions regarding War Diaries and Intelligence Summaries are contained in F.S. Regs., Part II. and the Staff Manual respectively. Title Pages will be prepared in manuscript.

Place	Date	Hour	Summary of Events and Information	Remarks and references to Appendices
Trenches	3/7/16		[sketch map showing GLORY LANE, LEAVE ALLEY, FRANKFORT TR., MUNICH TR., BEAUCOURT TR.]	— = Bosche line — = British do •• = dm strong points •• = Bosche do ⊠ = Bn H. Qs ✗ = Greenpost established

Our objective is to capture the trench marked thus ▬▬ and establish posts at junction of Leave Alley. Zero time was 4.15pm. "A" Coy under 2/Lt SMITH & 1/2 under Cpl Starr did the attack, by 7pm we had taken 200 yds of the left of the L but had not entered the right of attack. Casualties were 2/Lt Smith killed & 2/Lt Q O'Rourke & any 95 other ranks wounded. We established a post marked ✗.

WAR DIARY or INTELLIGENCE SUMMARY

(Erase heading not required.)

Instructions regarding War Diaries and Intelligence Summaries are contained in F.S. Regs., Part II. and the Staff Manual respectively. Title Pages will be prepared in manuscript.

Place	Date	Hour	Summary of Events and Information	Remarks and references to Appendices
Originel line German trenches	24/11/16	9 a.m.	This morning the 8th Lincolns ((63rd Bde) relieved us in trenches at Beaumont Hamel & we proceeded to Mailly 15 line Bosch line, where we rested for 2 hours & then continued on to Englebelmer.	P/V
ENGLEBELMER	25/11/16		Here we stay until 26th.	P/V
	26/11/16		N.L. Gr between 1/3 a good rest.	D/V
MAILLY MAILLET	26/11/16		To-day we marched from Englebelmer to Mailly-Maillet. We are in huts in Mailly wood.	P/V
ACHEUX wood	27/11/16		To-day we marched from Mailly Maillet to Acheux wood where the whole Battn is in huts.	P/V
"	28/11/16		N.L.	
"	29/11/16		Colonel Cobbold – has gone to take command temporarily of the 112th Bde and Lieut. H.S.A. ASKETT assumes (nominally) command of the Battn.	P/V
RUBEMPRÉ	30/11/16		To-day the Battn left Acheux wood at 6 a.m. arriving at Rubempré at 9.15 a.m.	D/V

WAR DIARY
or
INTELLIGENCE SUMMARY

(Erase heading not required.)

Instructions regarding War Diaries and Intelligence Summaries are contained in F.S. Regs., Part II. and the Staff Manual respectively. Title Pages will be prepared in manuscript.

Place	Date	Hour	Summary of Events and Information	Remarks and references to Appendices
RUBEMPRÉ	30/11/16		at Rubempré at 1pm. - Route, Beauval, Toutencourt, Herrisart. Men marched very well. 2/Lt. SMITH & 2/Lt. Millar joined on the 23rd inst. Lieut. Packett returned from the Base. To-day 2/Lieuts. - FINCH and HUGHES joined the Battn.	Est. Est. Shores next (a.g.) 10" howe. North haven St.
	30/11/16			

REPORT re - Fifth Army SG 72/94
V Corps No. GX 8418
<u>37th Division No. G. 1064.</u>

I was ordered to attack and take MUNICH TRENCH and FRANKFORT TRENCH on the morning of the 15th November. I was under the orders of B.G.C. 99th Brigade with whom I previously discussed the plan, an Artillery Group Commander, Colonel Goschen being present.

My orders were that an intense barrage would be put on MUNICH TRENCH from 9.0 am to 9.6 am and that the Heavies would bombard FRANKFORT.

I asked for a medium barrage to be placed in MUNICH from 8.20am to keep down the heads of the enemy whilst I formed up and advanced. This was promised.

My battalion formed up outside BEAUMONT Trench with left on CRATER TRENCH and advanced at 8.35 am on a true Easterly bearing the direction <u>by the left</u> being taken by compass.

We suffered some casualties from MG fire whilst forming up on the high ground.

No casualties occurred till after reaching WAGON Road when as my centre and right emerged from the sunken WAGON Road three shrapnel and one heavy shell burst in our midst - one group was annihilated by the big shell and the company suffered heavily from the shrapnel.

We still advanced suffering all the time from our light barrage till at about 8.55am the battalion arrived in a trench - mostly connected shell holes lying 150 yards due West of and parallel to MUNICH. Here we were caught by the 6 minutes intense barrage behind which we retired 50 yards and reformed. We lost at this trench almost entirely from our own barrage 8 officers killed out of 15 - 6 wounded and approximately 170 men.

The surviving Company Commander afterwards saw some A. and S. Highlanders in LEAVE ALLEY who had seen the whole affair and they declared our barrage was so short that not even a splinter would have reached MUNICH.

If it is contended that we ran into our intense barrage there could have been no medium barrage increasing in intensity from 8.20 am as promised.

After reforming the battalion under the one surviving officer who rallied with him elements of the 8th E. Lancs we again advanced, but the barrage was then well away and MUNICH was lined with men and machine guns, so the trench could not be carried.

I accompanied the battalion for some distance and later watched the battalion advancing from WAGON Road and I saw no German shells bursting, their barrage which was not heavy being directed on BEAUMONT Trench and the old German second line.

The morning was foggy.

                                      sd/ R. P. Cobbold, Lt-Col.
                                      Comdg 10th Loyal N.Lancs,
Nov. 22nd.   37th Divn.

<u>SECRET</u>.   BM X 57

Headquarters 37th Division.

Report called for in V Corps GX 8418 of 21st inst is forwarded herewith.

Lt-Col. R. C. Cobbold commanded the 10th L.N.Lancs during the attack on the 15th inst.

The barrage hampered this battalion on Nov. 15th between WAGON ROAD and MUNICH TRENCH between 8.45 and 9.6 am but especially during the intense barrage between 9.0 and 9.6 am.

                                      sd/ P.M.Robinson, Brig-Gen.
22. 11. 16.   Comdg 112th Inf. Bde.

37th Division No. G. 1086.

SECRET

V Corps.

Reference your GX 8418 dated 21/11/16, I forward herewith a report from the O.C., 10th Bn. L. N. Lancs Regt, 112th Inf. Bde; this Brigade on the day in question (15th November), was under the orders of G.O.C., 2nd Division.

With reference to your G.602, no information can be given regarding the 97th Inf. Bde, which forms part of the 32nd Division.

Adv. Headquarters
24. 11. 16.

Major-General
Commanding 37th Division.

SECRET.
　　　　　　　　　　　　　　　　　　Fifth Army SG 72/94
　　　　　　　　　　　　　　　　　　V Corps No. GX 8418
　　　　　　　　　　　　　　　　　　37th Division G.1064

V Corps.

　　　　Reports have been received that the attacks upon the MUNICH TRENCH by the 37th and 32nd Divisions were both hampered by our artillery barrage.

　　　　It has been stated that the 10th L.N.Lancs suffered from our own artillery fire, and that the 97th Brigade could not advance in places because the barrage was not on the trench, but some distance in front of it.

　　　　It is very necessary to investigate these reports thoroughly, both to ensure that the mistakes, if any, do not occur again, and to establish confidence.

　　　　Please furnish a report as early as possible.

　　　　　　　　　　　　　　　　sd/ C. N. MACMULLEN, Lt-Col.
21st November 1916.　　　　　　　　for Major-General GS

37th Division.
----

1. Ref. Fifth Army SG 72/94 of 21st inst, the GOCRA will investigate and forward report on the cases mentioned.

2. 32nd and 37th Divisions will forward for investigation report on any cases, other than the above, in which the infantry attack is stated to have been hampered by our barrage.
　　　　These reports to reach Corps H.Q. tomorrow, the 22nd inst.

　　　　　　　　　　　　　　　　sd/ F. W. Lumsden, Major.
　　　　　　　　　　　　　　　　　for B.G.,G.S.
　　　　　　　　　　　　　　　　　　　V Corps.

112th Inf. Bde.

　　　　Forwarded for report, please.

　　　　With reference to above, the following telegram from V Corps has been received.

" When forwarding report called for in V Corps GX 8418 of 21st November Divs will state date time and locality where the barrage hampered our troops and also the unit which was so hampered. 37th. Div. will state date time and locality with regard to the 10th. L.N. Lancs. and 97th. Inf. Bde. which was mentioned in Fifth Army S.G.72/94 forwarded under my G.X.8418 of 21st. inst. Addsd. 32 Div. and 37 Div."

　　　　　　　　　　　　　　　　　　　　　　Lt. Colonel.
Adv. Headquarters.　　　　　　　General Staff, 37th. Division.
22/11/1916.

112th Inf. Bde. B.M. 321.

23 Nov.

B.G.C.,
    112th Brigade.

News to hand is that the attack was greatly impeded by machine gun fire from FRANKFORT & GLORY Trench. Severel of our heavies dropped short and our advance was much hampered thereby. The Officer Commanding the Right attacking party was early killed. The O.C. the Right consolidating party was also knocked out and is so far missing.

Both sides of the TRIANGLE were strongly held. Bomb fighting at close range took place. My left hand party has pushed the Bosche back to within 50 yards of LEAVE AVENUE, and is consolidating. They have asked for more bombs and S.A.A. which has been sent them.

It is reported that the trenches were impassable for passage inside them and I gather the enemy had constructed a strong point on the top - about half way up to the right side of TRIANGLE.

Machine gun fire from the NORTH is constant and heavy.

The state of the ground is a morass and it is impossible to say which is trench and which is shell hole.

The situation is in hand but it will be impossible to say where we are till daylight.

Posts have gone out to their old positions, strengthened extra as ordered.

The shelling tho' not so heavy makes it difficult to get about, and BEAUCOURT TRENCH is very much knocked in making it easier for the Bosche machine guns in FRANKFORT to annoy us.

       (sd) R.P.Cobbold, Lt-Col.
7.30 pm.   Comdg. 10th L.N.Lancs.

2.

Headquarters,
    37th Division.

On enquiry I do not think there is evidence to show that the heavy shells referred to were fired from our own guns. They may easily have been fired from the direction of GRANDCOURT.

The farthest point reached is approximately Q.6.b.7.1½. A barricade has been constructed at this point, and a second about 40 yards out side of it. The second is a strong one with fire steps in it.

There is also a barricade at the S.E. corner

of THE TRIANGLE at the junction of the EASTERN and WESTERN sides.

Nothing in the nature of a counter-attack by the enemy has yet been made and we hold today all the ground taken last night.

Considering that the operation was carried out by a battalion which (with the exception of one night) has been continuously exposed to the weather for 10 days and has suffered very heavy casualties, especially in officers, I consider that both men and officers showed grit and good fighting qualities.

24/11/16.

Brigadier-General.
Commanding 112th Infantry Brigade

112th Brigade.
37th Division.

1/10th LOYAL NORTH LANCASHIRE REGIMENT

DECEMBER 1916

Army Form C. 2118

WAR DIARY
or
INTELLIGENCE SUMMARY
(Erase heading not required.)

Vol XVII

Place	Date	Hour	Summary of Events and Information	Remarks and references to Appendices
RUGEMORE	1/12/16		The Battn had a thorough kit inspection.	2Lt
"	2/12/16		Reorganisation of the Battn. Snipers, Bombers, Signallers & Lewis Gunners reformed. Colonel Caldwell returned from 112th Infy Bde.	2Lt
"	3/12/16		The following officers joined the Battn:- 2/Lt Willit Lieut Simpson " Crank " 2/Lt Reacon " Forresser " Goodman and 2/Lt Baker	2Lt
"	4/12/16		The Commanding officer lectured the officers of the Battn, and the Divisional Commander (Major-General Sir R Williams CB, DSO) came to listen.	5Lt 2Lt 3Lt
"	5/12/16		Ordinary Company work.	
"	6/12/16		2/Lt C T Roston returned from Hospital.	
"	7/12/16		Nil.	
"	8/12/16		The B.G.C. inspected the Battn — and viewed new places.	2Lt
"	9/12/16		Major Malcolm L Rose joined for duty as 2nd i/c.	2Lt
"	10/12/16			2Lt

Army Form C. 2118

WAR DIARY
or
INTELLIGENCE SUMMARY
(Erase heading not required.)

Instructions regarding War Diaries and Intelligence Summaries are contained in F.S. Regs., Part II. and the Staff Manual respectively. Title Pages will be prepared in manuscript.

Place	Date	Hour	Summary of Events and Information	Remarks and references to Appendices
RUBENPRÉ	11/12/16	10.30 a.m.	The V Corps Commander to inspect this Batln. tomorrow at Draft of 114 other ranks arrived last night. Further draft of 2 officers and 13 o.ranks arrived this evening. Bde. wires recd. at 11.30 a.m. to prepare to move to BEAUVAL & waiting Hon. by rail or road at short notice.	D/t. R/t.
"				
"	12/12/16		Corps Comdr's inspection cancelled. Orders received to move to 12th Bde. to be concentrated in the BEAUVAL area by the evening of the 13th inst. Our Army Bn. & Bde. Schools are closing & the students and staff returning. Haines & officers who joined 11-12-16 — 2/Lt IBBOTSON & 2/Lt Booth H.B.	D/t.
BEAUVAL	13/12/16	8.30 a.m.	At 8.30 a.m. the Batln. marched to BEAUVAL — to join the 1st Army. We arrived in Bon. billets at 12.15 p.m.	D/t.
BONNIÈRES	14/12/16		We marched from BEAUVAL to BONNIÈRES leaving the former at 8.45 and arriving at the latter at 3.30 p.m. Billets (not 1st rate good)	D/t.

Army Form C. 2118

WAR DIARY
or
INTELLIGENCE SUMMARY
(Erase heading not required.)

Instructions regarding War Diaries and Intelligence Summaries are contained in F.S. Regs., Part II. and the Staff Manual respectively. Title Pages will be prepared in manuscript.

Place	Date	Hour	Summary of Events and Information	Remarks and references to Appendices
ECOIVRES FRAMECOURT	15/7/16		We marched from BONNIÈRES to ECOIVRES leaving the (mes?) at 12.10 p.m & arriving here at 2.45 p.m. Two Companies are at Framecourt (1½ Kilometres away) and the rest of the Batt⁰ ao ECOIVRES. The C.O. went a (recce?) to day.	Slt.
BOUERS	16/7/16		At q. 10 am the Batt⁰ marched to BOUERS (N.W. of DIEVAL) thews billets good - Officers billets had. Distance 12 miles. 16 men fell out. Orders received at 11.30 p.m. to move at 9.20 am. B- morrow.	Slt.
HURIONVILLE	17/7/16		B⁰ marched off at 9.30 a.m. to-day via Pernes, Heringhen. Marched to Hurionville. Billets fair. Distance 8 miles, then fell out. Hurionville is just South West of LILLERS	Slt.
CARVIN Rebecque	18/7/16		The Batt⁰ left Hurionville at 8.45 a.m. and marched via Lillers to first Eaoty Rebecque - CARVIN.	Slt.
"	19/7/16		Orders received to march to Le Touret to-morrow.	
Le Touret	20/7/16		The Batt⁰ marched off at 9.15 am. via Hinge, Locon. 8 miles	Slt.

1875 Wt. W593/826 1,000,000 4/15 J.B.C. & A. A.D.S.S./Forms/C.2118.

WAR DIARY or INTELLIGENCE SUMMARY

Army Form C. 2118

Place	Date	Hour	Summary of Events and Information	Remarks and references to Appendices
2nd Turret	21/12/16		The Battn. here is in Support. B'de H.Qrs. are at Bethune. To-morrow the B'de goes into the line – Rue des Bois Sector – relieving the 15" H" Bdes, 5" Division.	Plts
Haystack Post (Hinges)	22/12/16		Relief commenced at 10 a.m. Our left two Companies i.e. C & D Coys took over from the 1st Devons whilst a third Coy i.e. A Coy took over from 1st R.W. Kents in Ht. Coy took up a hither to new position in Support to A Coy. Relief was completed by 1.45 p.m. We had to detail a new B"H.Qrs. which we did at Haystack Post. Great difficulty was experienced in laying down telephone lines etc. from two B.H.Qrs. (Devons & Kents) – and then they eventually our dispositions were more or less:–	

10th R Fusiliers ——— Are ——— Front line ——— 11th Bde

'C' Coy 4 platoons A Coy 2 platoons ——— Front line
'C' Coy 1 platoon ——— D Coy 4 platoons A Coy 2 platoons ——— in close Support
  B Coy 4 platoons ——— in Support

⊠ 15" Hd Qrs

8" East Lancs

N↑ S↓ W← E→

Army Form C. 2118

WAR DIARY
or
INTELLIGENCE SUMMARY
(Erase heading not required.)

Instructions regarding War Diaries and Intelligence Summaries are contained in F.S. Regs., Part II. and the Staff Manual respectively. Title Pages will be prepared in manuscript.

Place	Date	Hour	Summary of Events and Information	Remarks and references to Appendices
Trenches	23/12/16		Enemy quiet. Condition of trenches (breastwork) generally – good. Dug-outs = "Shanty". Wire = good in places. Everything else = trenches.	P/lt
"	24/12/16		At 12 noon to-day we commenced a slow intermittent gun fire on enemies front line trenches – in co-operation with the Trench Mortars, Lewis Guns, M. Guns & Snipers. This is to prevent fraternizing. Enemies retaliation failed to kill a N.C.O. & wound a Private.	C/lt
"	25/12/16		The Intermittent artillery fire became slightly more intense at "Stand- to". Enemy has so far shown no sign of leaving his trench – to fraternize!	S/lt
"	26/12/16		Enemy quiet.	P/lt
"	27/12/16		Orders received that 1st B. 6th Bedfs will relieve this B't. tomorrow.	C/lt. P/lt
"	28/12/16		Relief commenced at 12 noon was completed by 2.45 pm.	P/lt
Le Touret	29/12/16		The Bat'n furnishes are working parties for the Brigade. Open billets.	P/lt

WAR DIARY
or
INTELLIGENCE SUMMARY

(Erase heading not required.)

Army Form C. 2118

Place	Date	Hour	Summary of Events and Information	Remarks and references to Appendices
Le Touret	29/12/16		Are inadequate & had been rather unaided.	Elf.
"	30/12/16		Received draft of 150 o. Ranks & 5 officers.	Qu
"	31/12/16		Nil.	

Moore
Lieut & Q.
10th K.O. Lancs Rgt.

CONFIDENTIAL

WAR — DIARY 9of 18

10th (S) Bn Loyal North Lancs (R)

January 16th 1917 to January 31st 1917

Vol: No. XVIII

WAR DIARY
INTELLIGENCE SUMMARY
(Erase heading not required.)

Army Form C. 2118

Place	Date	Hour	Summary of Events and Information	Remarks and references to Appendices
L'Tower	1/1/17		Nil.	
"	2/1/17		The following officers joined the Battalion. 2/Lieuts Wage, 2/Lieuts: Roberts Bellis, Stonehouse Parker, Hobbs	96. 96.
Trenches	3/1/17		Colonel R. P. Cobbold, awarded the "Distinguished Service Order". This Batt. relieved the 6' Bedfds in the left Brigade Line Sector. Relief completed by 3pm. A Brigade School has been formed - each Battalion sends, 1 off., 1 C.S.M. and 136 other ranks, including 3 teams of Lewis gunners, 36 Bombers and the remainder are made up of "generally unwanted + backward men." School is situated at ROCQN.	96. 96. 9ft.
Trenches	4/1/17		Enemy very quiet. Lieut + Adjutant F. Howen awarded the Military Cross.	9ft.
"	5/1/17		Nothing to report	
"	6/1/17		Cpl Beaden Mentioned in dispatches - also Colonel Cobbold. D.S.O. Capt. W.H. PROCTOR, D.S.O. & Capt. O. Donovan R.A.M.C.	9ft. 9ft.
"	7/1/17		Nil.	
"	8/1/17			

WAR DIARY
or
INTELLIGENCE SUMMARY

Army Form C. 2118

(Erase heading not required.)

Place	Date	Hour	Summary of Events and Information	Remarks and references to Appendices
Le Touret	9/4/17		The 6" Beds A/S relieved the Batt. to-day. The 10" R.W. Fus. is the "resting" Battalion. Major Duncan appointed temporarily in command. Office at N. Staffs – Located 6" wh.	2/Lt.
"	10/4/17		Then an Fatted to-day	9/Lt.
"	11/4/17		Major T.D. Mayhew appointed 2nd in C. temporarily.	9/Lt.
"	12/4/17		Brig. General Riccardo, Cmg D.A. Lafettes Brigade, Command the 109" Bde. Colonel Cobbold D.S.O. of Th 2nd ashig B. & C. 112' Inf Bde until new General arrives – and Major Mayhew assumes temporary command.	
"	13/4/17		Following officers posted to this Battn: 2/Lieuts Logan, Cheetham Sear & Heyerick.	9/Lt.
"	14/4/17		Brig. General Macluchlan D.S.O. assumed Command of the 112 Bde. Colonel Cobbold A.D.S.S./Forms/C.2118. was given cmd of his Battn 9/Lt.	

WAR DIARY
or
INTELLIGENCE SUMMARY

Army Form C. 2118

Place	Date	Hour	Summary of Events and Information	Remarks and references to Appendices
Trenches	15/1/17		The Battalion relieved the 6. Bedf(rd) in trenches at 3 p.m. – Relief only took 2 hours to complete.	B.
"	16/1/17		A patrol went out last night – 2/Lt. & 9 O.Rs. – Saw 2 of the enemy on fence, as the true Cour d'Avoué – was there a bent at our patrol. Ground too totally unfit for patrolling.	Pt.
"	7/1/17		An attacking patrol consisting of 2/Lieut. S.B. SMITH 2/Lt. & 9 other ranks – went out at 11 p.m. returning at 2.30 a.m. The party went up to the enemy's wire to see if there was an entrance. As a large wire used gap was easily found 2/Lt. SMITH, Cpl Whittle & 2 officers went through the gap* and when within 3 yards of the enemy's parapet – an enemy in firing was shouted and immediately about 6 rifles blazed forth. 2/Lieut SMITH was wounded in 3 places but only slightly – Cpl Whittle was severely wounded in the thigh & has bullet through both his hands. The Patrol then returned, bringing * Remainder of party kept guard at the entrance*)	Plg.

WAR DIARY
or
INTELLIGENCE SUMMARY
(Erase heading not required.)

Army Form C. 2118

Place	Date	Hour	Summary of Events and Information	Remarks and references to Appendices
Trescoux	17/1/17		all the wounded back with them. Although this patrol was perhaps a little over cautious they brought back most important information — thus being that the gap in the wire was even covered by M.Gs, & Sentries.	B/r.
"	18/1/17		Nil.	B/r.
"	19.1.17		Quiet day. Lieut & A/Q. E. Newell is in Reserve Captain – Re Lt 19/6/17	Q/r. S/r.
"	20.1.17		Nothing unusual occurred	
"	21.1.17		Att. 6th Bedfords relieved this Batn in trenches relief being Complete by 3 pm.	B/r.
Pt Nuisset	22.1.17		Heavy Marganda reported for duty – from 3rd Lie Laws	B/r.
"	22.1.17		Att work parties furn each day – impossible to do any training	S/r.
"	23.1.17		Nil	B/r.
"	24.1.17		Nil	

Army Form C. 2118

WAR DIARY
or
INTELLIGENCE SUMMARY
(Erase heading not required.)

Instructions regarding War Diaries and Intelligence Summaries are contained in F. S. Regs., Part II. and the Staff Manual respectively. Title Pages will be prepared in manuscript.

Place	Date	Hour	Summary of Events and Information	Remarks and references to Appendices
Le Tanet	25/11/17		This Battalion has been detailed to make a raid of the Line Cour d'Avoué and Sourouris trenches on the morning of the 28th inst. There is a rough plan of the objective showing tracks etc.;	S/6.
"	26/11/17		The enemy shelled with 4.2s & 9s round Kingst. Little damage was done.	
"	27/11/17		Capt. C.O. Dannon. R.A.M.C. awarded the D.S.O. Cpl Burton the M.M.	S/6.

Place	Date	Hour	Summary of Events and Information	Remarks and references to Appendices
Lorient	27/4/17		2nd Lieut. Howard joined the Battn in the 21st. 21st Taylor on the 24/1/17. Capt. I A Grewett, M.C. joined on the 25/4/17. Major Lio Lucas, D.S.O, M.C. joined to-day as 2nd in C. 21sts Cliff & Sheridan joined since to-day. The Battn moved into Bde reserve area and are billeted at La Croix Marmuse.	S/L
La Cix Marmuse	28/4/17		This morning at 3am 3 parties each consisting of 1 offr & 23 other ranks entered the enemy trenches at Ferme Conin d'Avoue after a short bombardment. They entered the trench quite unmolested & secured 1 offr & 16 other ranks prisoners - approximately some 8 prisoner's earned a deal of trouble & were dealt with. Our Casualties were 3 other ranks killed & 2 missing & 11 other ranks wounded. No officers wounded. The enemy retaliation was feeble	D/L

WAR DIARY
or
INTELLIGENCE SUMMARY

(Erase heading not required.)

Army Form C. 2118

Place	Date	Hour	Summary of Events and Information	Remarks and references to Appendices
La Cx Mannien	29/1/17		NIL.	
"	30/1/17		Parades under Company arrangements.	
"	31/1/17		Orders received that the 31st Division are to be withdrawn from the line and be taken into GHQ & reserve. Gheghu Stores & transport lines are to move further out to this village to-morrow the 1st by 2pm from dawn on the 3rd prox: We are to be prepared to move at 6 hours notice.	

Ulman.
Capt & adjt
10th Bn Lancs Fus.

CONFIDENTIAL Vol 19

WAR — DIARY

of the

10th (S)(B)n. LOYAL NORTH LANCs

from JUN 1st 1917 to JUN 28 1917

VOL. XIX

Army Form C. 2118

WAR DIARY
or
INTELLIGENCE SUMMARY
(Erase heading not required.)

Instructions regarding War Diaries and Intelligence Summaries are contained in F.S. Regs., Part II. and the Staff Manual respectively. Title Pages will be prepared in manuscript.

Place	Date	Hour	Summary of Events and Information	Remarks and references to Appendices
La CROIX MARMUSE	1st Feb 1917		A new organisation for a platoon has been introduced which makes a platoon entirely self contained — for the next few days being in GHQ reserve we are to devote all attention to this new formation.	Pls Dr.
—do—	2/2/17		Nil.	
—do—	3/2/17		Colonel R.P Colville, RFO. Comdg- is going to BOULOGNE tomorrow an 8 days course of lectures etc.	Pls
—do—	4/2/17		Major J.D. MAYHEW (4th Middlesex) assumes Command of the Battn.	Pls Dr.
—do—	5/2/17		Nil.	
—do—	6/2/17		Orders received that the 8th Division is going down to the R to R Salient — to relieve the 24th Division, 1st Corps.	Pls Dr.
—do—	7/2/17		The C.O. & Coy Cmdrs Offrs go in buses to morrow to reconnoitre the line at HOOG —	Pls
—do—	8/2/17		Nil.	Pls Ply

WAR DIARY
INTELLIGENCE SUMMARY

Place	Date	Hour	Summary of Events and Information	Remarks and references to Appendices
Le Cix-Mannier	9/2/17		Orders received that the 112th Bde will tomorrow morning march to Les Brebis area — Starting point South of Bethune.	
Les Brebis	10/2/17		Bath of this Brigade marched at 2 am hour interval, order Eastfam, 10th Lours, Bedfords, Hi' Warwicks — Route: Zelobes, Locon, Bethune, Noeux-les-Mines — Les Brebis — At Les Brebis that Batt became Bn in Brig reserve & relieving the 13th MX Bn in billets.	
Hots (Hachetts)	11/2/17		This morning at 10 am, we started to relieve the 9th Royal Sussex Regt in Trenches. Relief was complete by 2:35 p.m.	
— do —	12/2/17		The enemy minenwerfer and MG fire was heavy during last night and his snipers were very persistent at "stand to" this morning. We suffered 1 killed & 5 wounded including one officer. This Batt. holds from the two craters inclusive to B5(c.4)H.31 8 9ao7 hence are on our right & the 4th Mx. (63rd RdDe) on our left. We have two Cos in the line and two Cos in Support — the Cos	

WAR DIARY
or
INTELLIGENCE SUMMARY
(Erase heading not required.)

Army Form. C. 2118

Place	Date	Hour	Summary of Events and Information	Remarks and references to Appendices
Loos Trenches	12/2/17		in support are in cellars in the "Enclosure" (not outside Loos.	Plt
"	13/2/17		Lt Col Colvered D.S.O. returned & assumed command again. 2/Lt. RE Quesnel joined for duty from the 1st British. The right wire guete. The left Coy which holds the Crassier have been told to do some wiring round the end of the Crassier as it is a vulnerable point.	P/St. P/St.
"	14/2/17		Nothing to report. Night passed quietly.	P/St. P/St.
"	15/2/17		Enemy last night threw several bombs into his own wire - He seems a bit nervy.	P/St.
"	16/2/17		The 6th Bedfordshire 1st relieve this Batt to-morrow.	P/St.

WAR DIARY
or
INTELLIGENCE SUMMARY

Army Form C. 2118

Place	Date	Hour	Summary of Events and Information	Remarks and references to Appendices
MAROC	17/2/17		To-day the 6th Bedfords relieved the Battn. in trenches and we withdrew to Maroc. Three Coys are in billets and one Coy. in St James & Trenin Keeps. Shaw has commenced any trenches toors on a deplorable state. Number given admitted to Field Ambulance Sick, Six & 10 men. Number of Wounded 20 + 3 killed.	
"	18/2/17		Work parties found by this Battn. number 370 O.Rks. 2/Lieut W.R. CROSSLEY, joined the Battn. for duty, from the 4th Loyal North Lancashire Rgt.	9/L
"	19/2/17			9/L
"	20/2/17		At 4.30am this morning a "Dummy" raid was carried out near Hurrians Hunts Crater. For 5 minute 4 batteries of 18 pdr three batts of H.5 fired at the	9/L

WAR DIARY
or
INTELLIGENCE SUMMARY
(Erase heading not required.)

Army Form C. 2118

Place	Date	Hour	Summary of Events and Information	Remarks and references to Appendices
MAROC	20/7/17		front line at Zero + 10 minutes lifted to the support line moving about barrage, Zero + 12 all guns returned to front line – in the life of catching enemy Standing to. There was very little retaliation.	
"	21/7/17		Nothing to report.	
"	22/7/17		Trenches have become drier in parts also –	
Suos.	23/7/17		To-day the Battⁿ relieved the 6th Bedfords – in trenches – Owing to the bad state of the trenches we relieved by platoons at 20 x interval – Relief commenced at 5pm and was complete by 8.35 pm. We had 5 men wounded by M G fire –	

WAR DIARY
INTELLIGENCE SUMMARY
(Erase heading not required.)

Army Form C. 2118

Place	Date	Hour	Summary of Events and Information	Remarks and references to Appendices
Fauchee	24/2/17		Quiet night - Some ammunition wagons fell into our lines during the may -	S/r.
"	25/2/17		Enemy very active with rifle grenades and aerial darts - they are very accurate with the later - Last night there was a heavy duel of Artillery fire and T.M. fire from both sides - first result of the double crossings -	S/r.
"	26/2/17			S/r.
Les Brebis	27/2/17		This Batt'n was relieved in trenches by the 6' Berkshires and withdrew to Divisional Reserve in Les BREBIS.	S/r.
"	28/2/17		Orders received that the 37 Division will be relieved by the 6. Division	

E.M.Nen. Capt + adjt
10 Hampshire Lancas B

112th Bde

Herewith War Diary for
March 1917, made up to date

E H Banks
Lt Colonel
10th L N Lancs

31/3/17

WAR DIARY or **INTELLIGENCE SUMMARY**

Army Form C. 2118

10 L N Lancs Vol 20

Place	Date	Hour	Summary of Events and Information	Remarks and references to Appendices
Le Ruitz	1/3/17		The Battalion is relieved by the 1st Buffs and marches to Bethune. Companies are billets in Montmorency Barracks.	2WRW
Bethune	2/3/17		Marched to Robecq for two nights. Very poor billets for the men.	
Robecq	3/3/17		Companies carry on with the new organisation of Platoons. A draft of 4th men from England arrive.	
Robecq	4/3/17		Batt. moves to St Hilaire, with the East Lancashire Regt.	
St Hilaire	5/3/17		Batt. again takes the road for Laires. Commanding Officer 2nd in C. Comp. Comm. & 1 officer per Coy proceed to Rainbert to witness a practice attack demonstrated by men of the 3rd Canadian Division.	
Laires	6/3/17		Battalion rests for one day. Time spent in carrying out the instructions as laid down in Batt. training.	
Laires	7/3/17		The Battalion on parade at 9.20 am and starts on the Road for Tangry. Arrive in Billets at 2.30 pm. Fairly good billets for the men.	

WAR DIARY
or
INTELLIGENCE SUMMARY

Army Form C. 2118

(Erase heading not required.)

Instructions regarding War Diaries and Intelligence Summaries are contained in F.S. Regs., Part II. and the Staff Manual respectively. Title Pages will be prepared in manuscript.

Place	Date	Hour	Summary of Events and Information	Remarks and references to Appendices
Saugny	8/3/17		The Battalion on the move at 8.15am again. This time for our destination ETREE-WAMIN. A long march of some 18 miles. but marching on the whole is very good – only two fell out. The men are in good form. Arrive in Billets about 5pm. Inhabitants not overjoyed to see us. Rations took evidently caused trouble.	
Etree Wamin	9/3/17		Company Commanders reconnoitre ground in the vicinity for Bombing and Assault courses. The men rest and clean up after 10 days marching.	
do	10/3/17		Companies took training according to instructions as laid down in the Memorandum of Battalion Training issued by the Commanding Officer.	
do	11/3/17		Church Parade service at 11.15am. for the whole Batt.	
do	12/3/17		Training continued. Lewis Gun, Bombing & Signalling Classes formed.	
do	13/3/17		Training goes on. – nothing of special note happens.	
do	14/3/17		Battalion Route march. Route Etree Wamin – Beauvoircourt – Grand Rullecourt – Canny – Etree Wamin.	JKBlaker

Army Form C. 2118

WAR DIARY
or
INTELLIGENCE SUMMARY
(Erase heading not required.)

Instructions regarding War Diaries and Intelligence Summaries are contained in F. S. Regs., Part II. and the Staff Manual respectively. Title Pages will be prepared in manuscript.

Place	Date	Hour	Summary of Events and Information	Remarks and references to Appendices
Noyelle Vermin	15/3/17		Still training. 2/Lt Roskrow is attached Lieutenant with Seniority from September 1916.	
do	16/3/17		Training carried on under Company arrangements.	
do	17/3/17		Brigade Route march at 9.25 a.m. arriving back at 1.45 p.m.	
do	18/3/17		Church Parade at 11.15 a.m. C.S.M. Whitaker is awarded the Italian Bronze Medal for Military Valour.	
do	19/3/17		Training goes on as usual. 2/Lt G.A. Goodman rejoins the Battalion and is posted as Second in Command of C. Company. Nothing of particular interest occurs. We carry	
do	20/3/17		usual work for exp. 3 Officers to reconnoitre areas.	
do	21/3/17		Still training. Capt. Howell is granted extension of leave.	
do	22/3/17		Again nothing to report. Three more officers sent to Arras.	2/Lt Blackh...

WAR DIARY or INTELLIGENCE SUMMARY

Army Form C. 2118

Place	Date	Hour	Summary of Events and Information	Remarks and references to Appendices
Etrun Warrus	23/3/17		Companies start training. Capt. Steel is attributed Hillas Agent but Corpls and is transferred to General Lecs. Brigadier views the Rest in Attack	
do	24/3/17		Battalion parades for Brigade Route March and returns about 1.30pm	
do	25/3/17		Church parade service at 11.15 am as usual. Usual football in the afternoon	
do	26/3/17		Training goes on. A platoon of B & C Coys give a demonstration before the Divisional Commander of "Platoons in the Attack" with Live ammunition and grenades. The General expresses himself as quite satisfied with work and commends the Battalion on its excellent discipline.	
do	27/3/17		Training as usual.	
do	28/3/17		ditto. Semi final of Brigade Football Competition takes place. We win. Also the final of the Boxing. We again win. Steel training. Lieut K.C. Watson joins the Battalion and takes over command of "A" Coy.	
do	29/3/17			
do	30/3/17		The Battalion parades for Brigade Operations which start at 12.25 pm at Licencourt. We gave over to B. Coy (?) in attack formation	

1875 Wt. W593/826 1,000,000 4/15 J.B.C. & A. A.D.S.S./Forms/C. 2118.11

WAR DIARY
or
INTELLIGENCE SUMMARY

(Erase heading not required.)

Army Form C. 2118

Place	Date	Hour	Summary of Events and Information	Remarks and references to Appendices
Bhee Wenirs	30/3/17	cont/	Everything seems to be undisturbed and is really an instructive exercise. The 10th LN Lancs are on the left in support to the East Lancs Regt. We get in touch will contact aeroplanes quite easily.	
do	31/3/17		Company training as usual, in the morning football in the afternoon.	

Approved
Lt Col
Commanding
10th Loyal N. Lancs

2/Lt Beauchamp-Wh--
4th Staff.
10th (S) Bn Loyal North Lancs Regt

112/37

Stewart Pte 21

Mrs Drew for
Above Pte
10th Loyal North Lancashire Regt

Army Form C. 2118.

WAR DIARY
or
INTELLIGENCE SUMMARY.
(Erase heading not required.)

Instructions regarding War Diaries and Intelligence Summaries are contained in F. S. Regs., Part II. and the Staff Manual respectively. Title pages will be prepared in manuscript.

Place	Date	Hour	Summary of Events and Information	Remarks and references to Appendices
ETREEWAMIN	1/4/17		We carry on with the training for offensive action.	Bn
do	2/4/17		Training – nothing of any interest to record.	Bn
do	3/4/17		Nil.	Bn
do	4/4/17		We are making final preparations for the offensive.	Bn
do	5/4/17		Recve orders that the 112th Bde will move to the forward area.	Bn
do	6/4/17		Battalion hands at 9.20 a.m. and goes into billets at Habarcq after a hard march. Evidence of great preparations all along the road.	Bn
Habarcq	7/4/17		We spend the night at Habarcq. Lt. Col. Owen A. Cameron of the Lincolnshire Regt joins as Second in Command. Major W. Moody informs the 8th Lincolnshire Regt. The final orders as to our objective are received. We are the Reserve Division to the VI Corps composed of the 3rd, 12th, 15th and 37th Divisions. The objective for this Division is a line drawn 1000 yds east of Monchy reaching the Cambrai Road. (As attached)	Bn
Habarcq	8/4/17	At 11.30 a.m.	Battalion moves to Wailly. The men are under Canvas here. Fortunately the weather is fine. Lt. Col. R.P. Oldfield goes to England for a rest and Lt. Col. O. A. Cameron assumes command.	Bn

WAR DIARY
or
INTELLIGENCE SUMMARY.
(Erase heading not required.)

Army Form C. 2118.

Instructions regarding War Diaries and Intelligence Summaries are contained in F.S. Regs., Part II. and the Staff Manual respectively. Title pages will be prepared in manuscript.

Place	Date	Hour	Summary of Events and Information	Remarks and references to Appendices
Maulio	8/4/17		cont. The following Officers are detailed to go into action. The Commanding Officer (The Adjutant) 2nd Lieut Blakeway (S.O.) 2nd Routh (I.O.) with Head quarters. Lieut R.E. Watson 2nd Deacon 2nd Waye with "A" Coy. 2nd Goodman 2nd Parker and 2nd Logan with "B" Coy. Capt. N.S. 2nd Prickett 2nd Strahan 2nd Cliff 2nd Aneuril with "C" Coy. Capt. 2nd Grant 2nd Bracewell 2nd Crosby 2nd Sheridan with "D" Coy. 2nd Lt Watt and 2nd R.A Storehouse are in charge of 100 men as carrying party.	Enc
Arras	9/4/17	4.10am	Batt moves to equipment dump West of Arras arriving at 6.20 am. The companies drew Bombs, Very lights, Tools, Iron Rations, Rifle Grenades etc. A hot meal was served from the Cookers and all stood by in readiness to move forward.	Enc
Arras	9/4/17	10.30am	Orders received to advance to the Assembly trenches in ICELAND Street	Enc
Arras	9/4/17	11.50am	Arrived at ICELAND Street and got into formation for attack. The Battalion was in support to the 6th Bedfords and 8th East Lancs	Enc
"	9/4/17	12.50pm	Battalion moved off in Artillery formation supporting the two above	Enc

WAR DIARY
or
INTELLIGENCE SUMMARY.
(Erase heading not required.)

Army Form C. 2118.

Place	Date	Hour	Summary of Events and Information	Remarks and references to Appendices
Arras	9/4/17		cnt. named Battalion. After having proceeded ½ mile, we made a flank movement to the left, crossing the CAMBRAI Road, then advanced eastwards, our right resting on 100 yards north of Road formation being as follows:-	
			'C' Coy Right front Company	
			'D' " Left "	
			'B' " In Support	
			'A' " In Reserve	
			H.Q. Coy.	
			We moved in above formation until we reached the slope upon which was the "BLUE LINE" System, see map attached, where we arrived about 4 p.m.	
			On still further advancing we came under Machine Gun fire, which was not deemed heavy enough to warrant a further extension, and continued to a line one parallel and 150 yards west of Road Running North from Feuchy Chapel Redoubt.	

WAR DIARY
or
INTELLIGENCE SUMMARY.
(Erase heading not required.)

Army Form C. 2118.

Instructions regarding War Diaries and Intelligence Summaries are contained in F. S. Regs., Part II. and the Staff Manual respectively. Title pages will be prepared in manuscript.

Place	Date	Hour	Summary of Events and Information	Remarks and references to Appendices
Arras	9/4/17		Cont. Having reached this line, the two front and supporting Companies dug themselves in, facing east, whilst the Reserve Company occupied two strong points immediately South of CAMBRAI Road. The recent A.Q. and 2 Lewis Guns teams established themselves in the vicinity of MAISON ROUGE.	RW
do	10/4/17	3.30am	We received orders to temporarily withdraw to allow 35th Brigade to get into battle formation previous to attacking 'BROWN LINE'. We withdrew to about ½ mile due West where we established ourselves in trenches, taking all due precautions and Lein ourselves in readiness to continue the advance.	RW
do	do	1pm	We continued our advance on to the 'BROWN LINE'. Here we were temporarily checked.	RW
do	do		On again advancing, being still in support to East Lancs and Bedfords, we were subjected to heavy barrage of Artillery & M.G. fire, owing to which we resorted to full extension	RW

WAR DIARY
or
INTELLIGENCE SUMMARY.
(Erase heading not required.)

Army Form C. 2118.

Place	Date	Hour	Summary of Events and Information	Remarks and references to Appendices
Arras	10/4/17	cont.	On reaching a line approximately running North and South through centre of N 6 c into N. 12 Central, the leading Battalion was checked under a burst in some dead ground between Contour 105 and 110 N. 6 d. and between contour 100 and 95. N. 12 c. On perceiving the enemy entrenched between Contours 105 and 110 N. 6 d. and contemplating a temporary 'stale mate', instructions were sent to the Reserve Coy. (Lieut Mabson) to swing North Eastwards and entrench themselves in the down slope between Contours 85 and 90 (M. 5. a.) It was here that 2/Lt Queenel was wounded. In order to protect the left flank and at the same time to enfilade any counter attack which might be made upon the S.W. East Lancs Left flank, the two Reserve Lewis Guns were brought to a commanding position where Contour 90 cuts Cambrai Road (N.11.A.B). After the Reserve Company had half sung themselves in,	EMc EMc

WAR DIARY
or
INTELLIGENCE SUMMARY.
(Erase heading not required.)

Army Form C. 2118.

Place	Date	Hour	Summary of Events and Information	Remarks and references to Appendices
Crrd	10/4/17	Cont.	A request was received from East Lancs to send a company to support their two left companies. At the same time a message was received from Capt. Garrett informing us that he was already supporting the two left companies of the East Lancs. with D/Coy under himself, whilst 'C' Coy under Capt Roskell was supporting the two right Coys. - the whole acting cover behind two banks on the rising contour (N.6.c & N.12.a.) 2nd Lieut. Goodman who was in command of the second wave, perceiving there was a big gap between the two left and two right Coys of the East Lancs, received to fill this gap. Therefore 'A' Coy. was taken from its work of protecting the left flank and sent forward to support the two left Coys of the East Lancs. It was now getting dusk. So the two Battalions, 10th L.F. Lancs and 8th East Lancs, dug themselves in and prepared for the night, having been reinforced by the Machine Gun Coy.	All EW

WAR DIARY
or
INTELLIGENCE SUMMARY.
(Erase heading not required.)

Army Form C. 2118.

Instructions regarding War Diaries and Intelligence Summaries are contained in F. S. Regs., Part II. and the Staff Manual respectively. Title pages will be prepared in manuscript.

Place	Date	Hour	Summary of Events and Information	Remarks and references to Appendices
Arras	11/4/17		During the night orders were received that the 1st L. Lancs. were to continue the advance and attack at 5 a.m. going through East Lancs. and attacking the trenches, having as our objective the "GREEN LINE" and in particular the work in O.S. Central	EE
do		5 am	The Battalion, having seriously got into position for such advance, almost immediately came into full view of the enemy and was met with very heavy machine Gun and Shell fire.	EE EE EE
do		5.30 am	We received orders not to advance until barrage opened. By this time, we had carried by assault, the Enemy trench in front (East of Sunken Road) and were establishing ourselves. Shell holes 100 yards further East. It was at this time that Capt. Robert W. Malcolm Woodman was killed. During this assault, we suffered very heavy casualties and were being enfiladed from Monchy Rd Front. The Right Flank, perceiving that they were in the air and appreciating the fact that if it remained as such, there was a likelihood of their being outflanked, boldly determined to not all and	EE

WAR DIARY
or
INTELLIGENCE SUMMARY.

Army Form C. 2118.

Place	Date	Hour	Summary of Events and Information	Remarks and references to Appendices
Arras	11/4/17		cont. assault a small trench running Southwards from CAMBRAI Road in the direction of GUEMAPPE and about 30 yards East of Sunken Road before mentioned. A Tank apparently also appreciating the situation in a like manner, came to their aid. On obtaining possession of the trench Corpl Lenard and L/c. R Brisarde and all men were all that was left. These eight men boldly bombed along the trench Southward killing more than a dozen Bosche, taking 3 prisoners and found themselves in complete possession. To their utter surprise, 1 Bosche officer miraculously appeared, apparently from nowhere. This was not a time to stand on ceremony, whereupon the officers suffered the same fate as their men. Two Machine Guns were captured in this gallant assault but as the new garrison were so weak in numbers and fearing	EM

WAR DIARY
or
INTELLIGENCE SUMMARY.

(Erase heading not required.)

Army Form C. 2118.

Place	Date	Hour	Summary of Events and Information	Remarks and references to Appendices
Arras	11/4/17		The Commanding Officer and Adjutant having collected en route stragglers of all Battalions to the number of about 50, arrived on the scene. By this time and with the assistance of these reinforcements, Capt. Garett was the complete master of the situation. From this time onwards, reinforcements of officers and men from other Battalions kept arriving.	Etc
do	do	1.30 p.m.	The Commanding Officer sent in a report to the General informing him that the situation had improved considerably and he had made plans for bombing parties to proceed along both sides of the CAMBRAI Road and to attack the enemy trenches after nightfall, which was about 300 yards in front of our line as it was not deemed advisable at that moment to advance further, knowing full well that we were well in advance of all troops on our Right and Left, besides, which, in our present position we had command of a good field	Etc

WAR DIARY
or
INTELLIGENCE SUMMARY.
(Erase heading not required.)

Army Form C. 2118.

Place	Date	Hour	Summary of Events and Information	Remarks and references to Appendices
Arras	11/4/17		that they might eventually be in their turn encircled, they blew them up. These men retained possession of this trench as did also Capt. Garrett, ably assisted by 2nd Lt. Deacon (being the only two officers now left) and C.S.M. Webster with 60 men, made themselves masters of the situation of the corresponding trench running northwards from the CAMBRAI Road. Here the garrison remained throughout the day, although there were signs of the enemy massing for a counter attack from the South. I was about this time hit by Parker died after being During this period 2/Lt. Deacon received two wounds, but badly wounded would not desert his Captain or his men. About 3 hours after entering the trench, some of the 3rd Dragoon Guards, acting as Infantry, came up on their left. This gave them some breathing space. During this time men of the East Lancs and 10th R.S. Lancs CM oozed from shell holes and thickened the line.	CM

WAR DIARY
or
INTELLIGENCE SUMMARY.
(Erase heading not required.)

Army Form C. 2118.

Place	Date	Hour	Summary of Events and Information	Remarks and references to Appendices
Arras	11/4/17		Cont. of fire to our front line and could also enfilade the enemy on our right where the troops on that flank would advance further.	EVE
do	do	5pm	We received orders that we would be relieved at 6.30 p.m. & immediately informed Capt. Gravett to hold himself in readiness to be relieved. This relief was not complete until 1 a.m. of the men, being in a very exhausted condition withdrew to Telegraph Wood we spent the remainder of the night.	EVE EVE
Telegraph Wood	12/4/17	8am	Roll Call. Only a few of the brave fellows left. Our losses went estimated at 13 Officers and 266 men, that is our 60% of our fighting strength.	EVE EVE
		11am	All that is left of the Battalion marches down the Cambrai Road and is billeted in Arras in cellars. We remained here until 4.30 am on	EVE
Arras	13/4/17		when the battalion was conveyed to lorries to Wanquetin for a days rest.	EVE EVE
Wanquetin	14/4/17	11.40am	Parade to march to Aubigny arrived at Him Excellent billets.	EVE EVE

WAR DIARY
or
INTELLIGENCE SUMMARY

(Erase heading not required.)

Army Form C. 2118

Place	Date	Hour	Summary of Events and Information	Remarks and references to Appendices
Ambrines	14/4/17		for the men. Which they richly deserve.	See
do	15/4/17		Cleaning up and generally a day of rest.	See
do	16/4/17		The Battalion starts to re-organise and prepare for the next offensive action which we all feel will not be long in coming.	See
do	17/4/17		Route March in the morning and training in the afternoon	See
do	18/4/17		We receive orders that we are to move the next day to Habarcq (the forward area) All possible preparations are made. A draft of 28 men are posted to the Batt.	See See
do	19/4/17		The division is transferred to the 17th Corps again and the battalion moves to Habarcq.	See
Habarcq	20/4/17		We remain here for the day and the Commanding Officer and Adj. reconnoitre to consider the line.	See

WAR DIARY
or
INTELLIGENCE SUMMARY.
(Erase heading not required.)

Army Form C. 2118.

Place	Date	Hour	Summary of Events and Information	Remarks and references to Appendices
Habarcq	21/4/17	7am	Move to St Nicholas in dugouts (N. of Arras) and relieve 1st Bn Royal Warwickshire Regt.	&c &c &c
St Nicholas	22/4/17		Remain here and draw fitting equipment of sorts and draw lots to rehearse for future operations. Coy Commanders again reconnoitre the line.	&c &c
St Nicholas	23/4/17	3am	Leaving our details and transport behind we move off & Railway cutting about 2 miles away and lay in Reserve waiting orders to move.	&c &c
		7am	We were off again in Artillery formation this time in Brigade Reserve. The Col. Bedfords are on the right 1st Royal Warwicks left. Each were in support and ourselves in Reserve. After passing through an unpleasant shrapnel barrage we eventually arrive in Laurel Trench suffering 5 casualties. Here we remained until 4.50 p.m. the afternoon. (These follow diary compiled by Lt Col Ewen A Cameron)	&c &c

T2134. Wt. W708-776. 500000. 4/15. Sir J. C. & S.

Army Form C. 2118.

WAR DIARY
or
INTELLIGENCE SUMMARY.
(Erase heading not required.)

Instructions regarding War Diaries and Intelligence Summaries are contained in F.S. Regs., Part II. and the Staff Manual respectively. Title pages will be prepared in manuscript.

Place	Date	Hour	Summary of Events and Information	Remarks and references to Appendices
			When we received orders to mass Chalk Trench and to be in readiness to advance and attack the Brown Hill from there	Que
		5.45 p.m.	The Battalion encountered heavy hostile Artillery fire on route suffering casualties	2cc
				2cc
				Cu
		6.p.m.	Our Artillery opened shrapnel barrage for 25 minutes then H.E. for 5 minutes. During this barrage we halted in a trench a short distance behind Chalk Trench, East Vaux's, being on our left.	
		6.30.p.m.	The Battalion to Chalk Trench. During this advance the Regiment suffered tremendously. Every Battalion got thoroughly shaken, Eighteen Doctors [?] being killed and only 3 Officers left, several etc. The Battalion halted to get to Blue Line, so crowded in shell holes etc. till dusk when I collected them together as best we could be done and fight it as a Unit in Chalk Trench but letting	Que

T2134. Wt. W708—776. 500000. 4/15. Sir J. C. & S.

my Right Flank with Lewis Guns and outposts from the direction of Lepenny and covering the Huchy Huchy with the other flank securing.

Sections of Machine Guns reinforced me and got into position on my flanks.

I detailed my Headquarters to small towers in front of Hypnaved Works (H.12.6.53) and established telephonic communication and formed a line.

Throughout the night the Battalion was subjected to heavy shelling.

Preparations were made for position to be ready by 2 a.m. when we relieved 63rd Brigade in Blue Line.

The attack which had taken place been carried out successfully by this Regiment on the 23rd was undoubtedly a failure due to its not being in readiness at considering the nature of the ground over which we had to advance, also owing to the

WAR DIARY
or
INTELLIGENCE SUMMARY
(Erase heading not required.)

Army Form C. 2118

Place	Date	Hour	Summary of Events and Information	Remarks and references to Appendices

Heavy Barrage of both Artillery and Machine Gunfire which "played" upon this ground. Furthermore, the Brigade which was in front, in my opinion, ought have given no proper support during our advance in the Blue Line, by keeping up a continuous fire which ought have related back some of the Enemy's Machine Gunfire etc.

The Officers and N.C.O's of this Battalion were magnificent in their endeavours to keep men together and to encourage their advance, but in spite of all endeavours in vain, I regret to say checked before reaching the Blue Line, so practically were unable to take Eversland Hill.

When I saw the seriousness of this check, there was nothing left to be done, but to collect as many men as possible and get them to a place of safety, and at the same time, to be of tactical support, this fire I chose the (trench, which was only a French en masse).

Place	Date	Hour	Summary of Events and Information	Remarks and references to Appendices
	25th		This we deepened and consolidated and were prepared to advance or to repel any attack on our Right flank which was more than probable owing to the Divisions on our Right having been held up until the Chemical Works was a very likely direction to expect trouble from. Held Chalk Trench as our forward line and a trench in Sunken Road as our Support line. Night fairly quiet.	
	26th		At 9 am a Boche plane flew low over our line. Machine Guns and Rifle fire was brought to bear on it with the result that it had to descend out of control in the German Lines. The day was fairly quiet except for about an hour onwards from 10·45 when an enemy aeroplane again flew over us and gave the lines as a target to his artillery.	

WAR DIARY
or
INTELLIGENCE SUMMARY

(Erase heading not required.)

Army Form C. 2118

Place	Date	Hour	Summary of Events and Information	Remarks and references to Appendices
		11.30 pm	suffered a few Casualties. 2/Lt. Roberts reconnoitred Cuba Trench and formed an occupied. He immediately established a Lewis Gun	
			Post and 2 bombing posts in it	
		4.20 am	The enemy were seen making their way from their hole to steel hole towards Cuba Trench. One ran shot by us, remaining 2 retired.	
			Remained all day as before. During night moved 2 Companies into Cuba and brought Leipzig & Inglaterra into new trench in front of Clash Trench.	
	2/7		Attended Conference at B.H.Q. He received orders to attack Leinster Trench at dawn next day. Made all the necessary arrangements and decided the Battalion should go over in two waves, in the meantime getting my platoon which was chiefly in Cuba, but into the open	

Army Form C. 2118

WAR DIARY
or
INTELLIGENCE SUMMARY
(Erase heading not required.)

Place	Date	Hour	Summary of Events and Information	Remarks and references to Appendices
	28th	4.20am	about 100 yards in front, so as to get a good start and escape any enemy fire which might be brought to bear on it, my second manoeuvering which it may. Barrage opened, Battalion being already in positions for attack. The enemy did not put up much of an artillery barrage so I immediately brought my second wave into new trench.	
		4.2?am	The Battalion attacked and reached a point where a trench had been begun by the enemy. By this time the Battalion had suffered heavily and only one Officer (2/Lt Jones) was left. The Battalion immediately commenced to dig in into this newly begun trench as they were so heavily enfiladed with Machine Guns from Right Flank (Chemical Works)	

WAR DIARY
or
INTELLIGENCE SUMMARY
(Erase heading not required.)

Army Form C. 2118

Place	Date	Hour	Summary of Events and Information	Remarks and references to Appendices
			There were several batches of the Regiment still further advanced in shell holes. These readily renewed their all day, sniping and doing as much damage as they could. By the time the Battalion was dug in, between 50-60 were all that remained. During the advance, a few of the East Lanes, Bedfords and Warwicks, joined my Battalion and dug in with us. This attack on Greenland Hill once more failed, although we did gain some ground. Undoubtedly the Chemical Works was the main reason for this failure, but I cannot help thinking that my Battalion had been supported in a more determined manner, we might have got to the enemy's trench, but they were so thin in numbers they were killed or wounded.	

WAR DIARY or INTELLIGENCE SUMMARY

Army Form C. 2118

Place	Date	Hour	Summary of Events and Information	Remarks and references to Appendices
	29/4/17	1am	There was a great delay and much confusion at the time of the start, amongst the Supporting Battalion which I myself interviewed and tried to rectify. I am afraid this delay was a great handicap to the leading Battalion as the wave which should have been the first evidently never started, or if it did, it didn't support my Battalion. Only the second wave appears to have got through, so naturally, there was a gap between the front wave and the supporting ones. Still on the whole, I am afraid the Right Flank was the main reason for our failure.	
		1am	The 10th Argyle and Sutherland Highlanders came up to relieve the 11/34 Bde. The Relief was completed by about 4am. When the remnants of the Batt. marched down to the Transport lines at St. Nicholas	
		3hm	We headed to be counted in lorries to Aubines where we	

WAR DIARY
or
INTELLIGENCE SUMMARY
(Erase heading not required.)

Army Form C. 2118

Place	Date	Hour	Summary of Events and Information	Remarks and references to Appendices
Aubers	29/4		Eventually arrived at 7 p.m.	2.OC
Aubers	30/4		The day was spent in clearing up and resting.	
			We estimate our casualties for these operations as 8 Officers killed and wounded. O. Ranks killed 19 wounded 112 Missing 18 making a total of 21 Officers and 498 Other ranks casualties during the operations on Moudy and Greenland Hill.	R.W

J. Cowdy

Lt. Col. Comdg.
10th Loyal North Lancashire Regt.

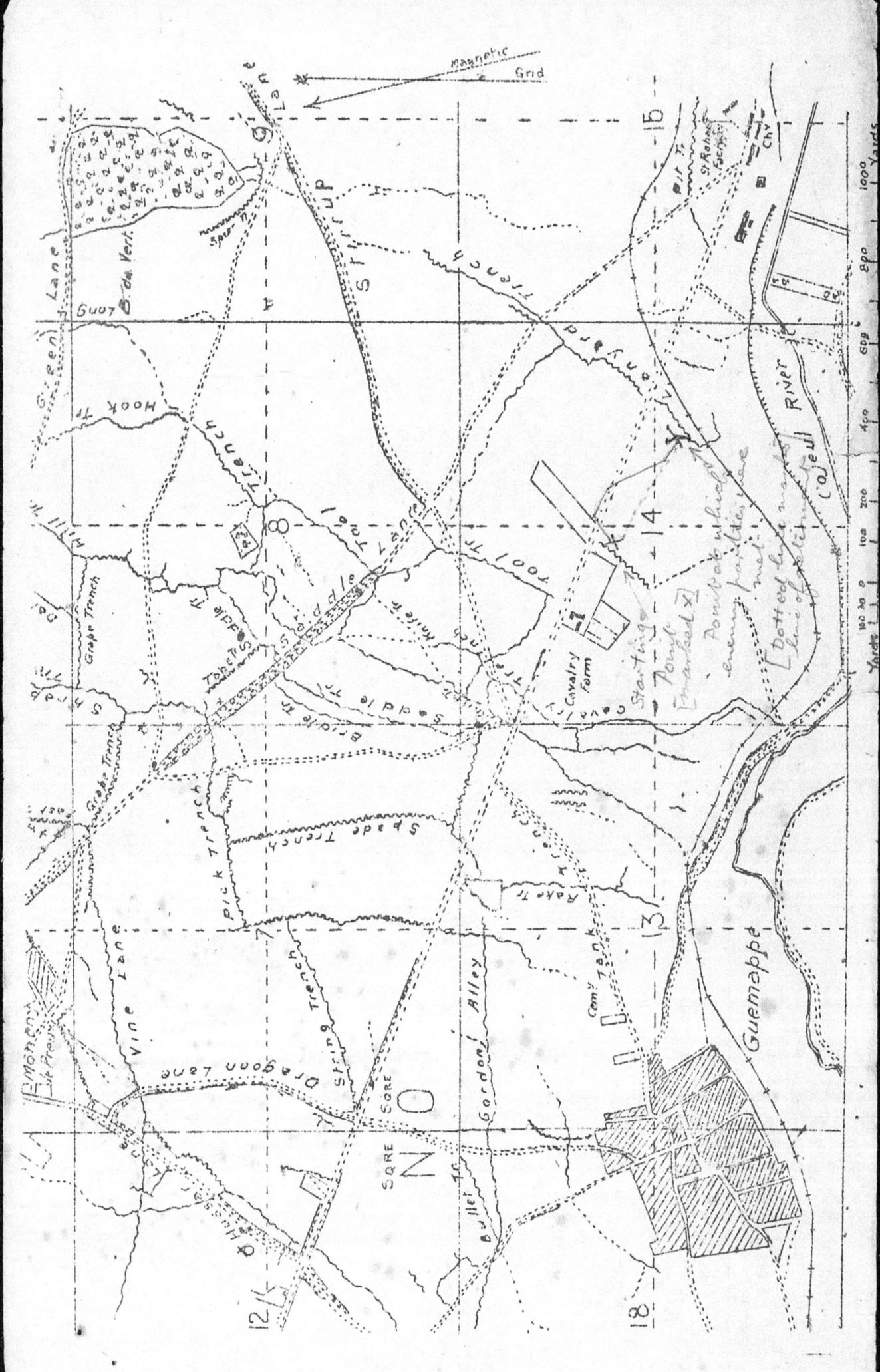

1/7th Loyal North Lancashire Regt

WAR DIARY
or
INTELLIGENCE SUMMARY

Army Form C. 2118

112/37

Vol 22

Place	Date	Hour	Summary of Events and Information	Remarks and references to Appendices
Rouen	1/5/17		Draft of 3 Officers and 134 O.R. arrive. Lt. R.E.A. Way, Lt. C.L. Kelly and Lt. P.S. Mangol au Johe from the artists Rifles.	See
do	2/5/17 to 5/5/17		2nd Lt. C. Brown is promoted Capt. Batt. begins training.	See
			Training in new Warfare each day	See
			Nothing of the rue interest is record.	See
do	6/5/17		Church Parade. Lt. J.C. Wright joins the Batt from 6th Yorkshire Regt	See
do	7/5/17		Batt. Training, Musketry for Brigade Musing and Field firing competition.	See
do	8/5/17		A day completes in Musing competition Co. by for the Field Firing do.	See
do	9/5/17 to 14/5/17		Battalion is still training in the area. Lt Col Esdaile of the K.O.R.L.R. joins as Second in command.	See

WAR DIARY
or
INTELLIGENCE SUMMARY
(Erase heading not required.)

Army Form C. 2118

Place	Date	Hour	Summary of Events and Information	Remarks and references to Appendices
Ambrines	18/5/17		Battalion moves from AMBRINES to MONTENESCOURT arriving about 2 p.m. where they remain for the day.	Eac.
Montens court	19/5/17	10 a.m.	Leave here for TILLOY where we relieve the 5th London Regt. L.R.B. in Shelters at 2.30 p.m. Here we remain until	Eac.
TILLOY	20/5/17	9 p.m.	when we moved up into Battalion in Reserve in VANCOUVER Line and = join the 13th K.R.R.C.	Eac.
Vancouver Line	24/5/17		Here we remain for 4 days finding Working parties at night and salvaging during the day.	Eac.
	24/5/17	10 p.m.	Relieve 11th Royal Warwickshire Regt on the right sub sector in front of GUEMAPPE.	Eac.
Guemappe	25/5/17		The following Officers join the Bat. Capt J.A. Grout, N.C. Lewis Wason, 2nd Lieut. J.R. Pidcock, 2nd Lieut. D. Watson & 2nd Lieut ? Quesnel.	Eac.

WAR DIARY or INTELLIGENCE SUMMARY

Army Form C. 2118

Place	Date	Hour	Summary of Events and Information	Remarks and references to Appendices
	26/6/17		2/Lt Booth took out a patrol consisting of 1 Pte. Taylor from hours O.8.c.9.2 (see map attached) at 12 midnight - they proceeded towards O.14.R.3.8 about 250 yds. Here they found shell holes joined by short lengths of trench. They were still being dug by the Boche and talking could be plainly heard. On the return of the patrol Lewis Guns were immediately opened on the area covered.	Enc Enc Enc Enc
	27/6/17		At 10 p.m. a patrol of 6 men went out to see if LANYARD trench was occupied. the enemy were found working in the trench. Starting (?) they found coming towards them two patrols of about 10 men each. Bombs were at once thrown and took effect but the patrol had to retire owing to greatly superior numbers. The same evening 2/Lt Booth again went out taking 2/Lt Nuttall and Pte Taylor with him. This was to identify 2 Boche moving by our critters (?)	Enc Enc

WAR DIARY
or
INTELLIGENCE SUMMARY
(Erase heading not required.)

Army Form C. 2118

Place	Date	Hour	Summary of Events and Information	Remarks and references to Appendices
			Passing over the ridge above O.8.d.1.1 (see map attached) they came across two dead Germans in a shell hole, both (whom) had been shot in the back, there seemed little doubt as to these being Germans shot in the morning. An search of each was cut off and proved that they belonged to the 414th Regiment of Foot. Having finished the task allotted to them they lay and watched the enemy's movements thereby being armed useful information. It was found that at 10.30pm the enemy occupied an organised line of shell holes manned by M.G's about O.14.B.c.8 & 4.4.6. The Patrol returned at 11.20pm	E.a.c. E.a.c.
28/5/17			Fairly quiet until 11pm when our line was heavily shelled. Capt MacNamara was wounded. Also 4th R.F.A. Way.	E.a.c.
29/5/17			During the night of 28/29 we were relieved by the 13th Royal Fusiliers. The Batt was billeted in Arras.	E.a.c.

Army Form C. 2118

WAR DIARY
or
INTELLIGENCE SUMMARY
(Erase heading not required.)

Place	Date	Hour	Summary of Events and Information	Remarks and references to Appendices
	2/5/17		cont. in SCHRAMM BARRACKS. Men were warned for the next day cleaning up and having inspection of equipment and clothing etc. The Batt. moves into DOISANS, arriving about 12.30 p.m. Billetted in huts.	

Swainson
Lt. Col. Comdg.
10th (S) Bn. Loyal North Lancashire Regt.

War Diary
10th LN Lancers
June 1917

No 23
SECRET

To
    Hd Qrs 112th Inf Bgde

Herewith WAR DIARY for the month of JUNE please

[stamp: ORDERLY ROOM, Date 1/7/17, LOYAL NORTH LANCS REGT.]

1/7/17

E.W.B. Holt
Lieut & Adjt
for LT. COLONEL
10th (S) Bn. THE LOYAL NORTH LANCASHIRE

Army Form C. 2118.

WAR DIARY
or
INTELLIGENCE SUMMARY. 10th Loyal North Lancashire Regt
(Erase heading not required.)

Instructions regarding War Diaries and Intelligence
Summaries are contained in F.S. Regs., Part II.
and the Staff Manual respectively. Title pages
will be prepared in manuscript.

Place	Date	Hour	Summary of Events and Information	Remarks and references to Appendices
Ousans	1/6/17		Coys are at the disposal of Coy. Commanders for reorganisation and training. The following Officers NCOs and men have been awarded as under	
			Capt. J.A. Gravett-Bor M.C. C.S.M. V. Webster M.C. Military Medals awarded to C.S.M.S. Lomas. L/Cpl. Chetham L/Cpl. Bibby T. Pte W. Wood	
			A/Cpl T.H. Maxfield, Pte T. Johnstone Pte E. Hall Sgt M. Doyle. A/L/C Hallwell	
			Pte A. Brown L/Cpl J.E. Wilcox L/cpl I. O'Connor, Sgt S.J. Simpkins L/cpl L. Salmon	
			Pte T. Harrison Sgt L. Lewis Pte L. Kavanagh	a/c
do.	2/6/17		Saturday, Divine Service is held as we march tomorrow, Evening is	a/c
			passed as usual.	
do.	3/6/17		Battalion moves to Villers-Sur-Simon at 5 A.M.	a/c
Illers-sur-	4/6/17		Train again on the old area in Ambrines. All employed men	a/c
Simon			on parade for Saluting drill. Lectures in the evening	a/c
do	5/6/17		Battalion training. The following officers joined the Batt to day. 2/Lt King W.C.H Hopcroft, J.H Anderson, LB Smith, G Bryson	
do	6/6/17		Brigade Orderlies - We attacked the Boche and held up the British attack	a/c
			an interesting and instructive exercise.	a/c
do	7/6/17		Battalion moves to VAL-HOUN + HUCLIER - a long tiring march very hot.	a/c

T2134. Wt. W708—776. 500000. 4/15. Sir J. C. & S.

WAR DIARY
or
INTELLIGENCE SUMMARY.

Army Form C. 2118.

Place	Date	Hour	Summary of Events and Information	Remarks and references to Appendices
cont	7/6/17		cont. Every man marches on interest. We pass many on the roadside. Some of the Royal Naval Service Reg.t however. The Battis are very worried but lucky we only stay one Night	
Militron	8/6/17		The Battalion marches to Capelle-air-la-Lys - Glenn and Nurcauville are Russos. Arrived about 1pm. Billets are quite good and clean.	exc
Capelle-sur-a-Lys	9/6/17		The necessity for having an Orderly officer is brought to our notice and one is instituted forthwith. Battalion to Thurnne	exc
do	10/6/17		Sunday This arrangement of having a day of rest, a third parade is impossible, all billets are inspected by the Commanding officer	exc
do	11/6/17		Corps Sunday sports at the training area for Rainnes according to programme drawn up.	exc
do	12/6/17		Coys training in area all day. Night Operations on Bedford trench for Platoons	exc
do	13/6/17		Battalion sports held in area for Brigade Sports on Sunday. Etc.	exc
do	~~14/6/17~~		Everything a great success	exc
do	14/6/17		Musketry Course begins with Sroving. Every man in the Battalion has to fire. Lt. M.J. Kay & 2/Lt. Bleyden Beckett join the Battalion.	exc

WAR DIARY
or
INTELLIGENCE SUMMARY.
(Erase heading not required.)

Army Form C. 2118.

Place	Date	Hour	Summary of Events and Information	Remarks and references to Appendices
Mahulsette	15/4/17		Early morning parades every day now for ½ hour. At 5 a.m. and continue course.	see
do	16/4/17		Coy work on the training area and on the Ranges in the afternoon. Orders received to discard our Divisional sign Yellow Triangle.	see
do	17/4/17		Church parade for Coys that are not firing. Musketry continues	see
do	18/4/17		Two companies on the range and the remainder each day do work. Brigadier starts a tactical tour for Commanding Officers and Adjutants. Amerin Singh majorly wounded at Mahulsette. Since in	
do	19/6/17		Two companies on the Range, and remainder on training area.	see
do	20/6/17		Coys work under Coy arrangements.	see
do	21/4/17		The following Officers Nos. were were the ribbon of thier awards at the heads of St General trooper. Commanding 1st Army. M FRUGES.	see

Capt. J.A. Grasett (Sub. 6) awarded Bar to M.6.6.
Lieut. H.L. Jones do do
2nd Lieut. C.J.M.B. 2nd Webster M.b.

WAR DIARY
or
INTELLIGENCE SUMMARY.
(Erase heading not required.)

Army Form C. 2118.

Place	Date	Hour	Summary of Events and Information	Remarks and references to Appendices
Lagnicourt sur le 2/17			Awarded Bar to M.C. 6. For conspicuous gallantry, indomitable courage and good leadership at Monchy le Preux on 11th April, 1917.	
			2 Lieut. H.L. Jones. awarded the Military Cross. For conspicuous gallantry and good leadership at GAVRELLE 28th April 1917, in leading his Battalion forward when all other officers were casualties.	
			14111 C. Sclt. J. Webster awarded the Military Cross. For conspicuous bravery, personal example and good leadership in taking command of two Companies at BEAUMONT HAMEL on 11th May, 1916 and again at MONCHY le PREUX on 11th April, 1917.	
			3879 L. Cpl. S.J. Lomax. awarded the Military Medal. For conspicuous gallantry and good leadership at MONCHY le PREUX on 17 April 1917, when in command of his company	2nd
			13708 Sgt. J. Lewis. awarded the Military Medal, For great devotion to duty and personal example at GAVRELLE. 28th April 1917.	2nd

WAR DIARY
or
INTELLIGENCE SUMMARY
(Erase heading not required.)

Army Form C. 2118

Place	Date	Hour	Summary of Events and Information	Remarks and references to Appendices
Chapelle du la Lys.	21.6.17		13375 Sgt. J. Leonard. awarded the Military Medal. For conspicuous gallantry in leading a bombing party which captured a German trench at LA BERGERE cross roads, 11th April, 1917.	
			14346 Sgt. W. Doyle. awarded the Military Medal. For great gallantry and good leadership when in command of his platoon in the attack on GAVRELLE 28th April. 1917.	
			16891 Cpl. J. J. Simpkins awarded the Military Medal. For coolness and devotion to duty in constantly repairing telephone lines under heavy fire at GAVRELLE on 28th April. 1917.	
			13460 Cpl. H. Halliwell awarded the Military Medal. For gallantry and devotion to duty in carrying messages under fire throughout the operations at GAVRELLE 28th April. 1917.	
			19704 L/c. J. J. O'Connor. awarded the Military Medal. For gallantry and devotion to duty doing great execution with his Lewis Gun at GAVRELLE on 28th April. 1917.	B.

WAR DIARY
or
INTELLIGENCE SUMMARY
(Erase heading not required.)

Army Form C. 2118

Place	Date	Hour	Summary of Events and Information	Remarks and references to Appendices
Opelle du la hyp.	21-6-17		22958 L/c E. Salmon, awarded the Military Medal for courage and devotion to duty at GAVRELLE on 28th April 1917, giving great assistance to the relieving Battalion with regard to the Lewis Gun posts. 21822. Pte. J. Bibby. awarded the Military Medal. for conspicuous bravery at MONCHY le PREUX on 11th April 1917, in working his Lewis Gun under heavy shell fire. 16773 Pte. H. Wood. awarded the Military Medal for great coolness and courage in working his Lewis Gun at MONCHY le PREUX 11th April 1917. 31813 Pte. J. Johnstone, awarded the Military Medal for great bravery and determination in taking charge of a Party bringing up rations through a heavy barrage at GAVRELLE 28th April 1917.	Eve

Army Form C. 2118

WAR DIARY
or
INTELLIGENCE SUMMARY
(Erase heading not required.)

Instructions regarding War Diaries and Intelligence Summaries are contained in F.S. Regs., Part II. and the Staff Manual respectively. Title Pages will be prepared in manuscript.

Place	Date	Hour	Summary of Events and Information	Remarks and references to Appendices
22/6/17	22/6/17		Receival the disposal of Coy Commanders. We get orders for the move to WITTES. and send billeting party in advance.	See
Capelle Sunday's				
WITTES	23/6/17		Battalion marches to WITTES. The men fall out. Arrive at 8 am	See
Hondeghem	24/6/17		Move to Hondeghem and arrive after a very trying march.	
Locre	25/6/17		March to LOCRE where we meet our 9th Battalion and are made welcome.	See
Locre	26/6/17		A day of rest. Cleaning up.	See
Locre	27/6/17		Batt. parades for inspection by C.O.	See
Locre	28/6/17		General Sir Herbert Plumer the Army Commander inspects the Brigade.	See
Locre	29/6/17		Brigade moves into Divisional Reserve and relieves 108th Bde. of 36th Div. near Kemmel.	See
Kemmel	30/6/17		The line is reconnoitred. Working parties are found for working on Reserve line.	See

R.G. Garnett Lt. Colonel Comde.
4th (S) Bn. THE LOYAL NORTH LANCASHIRE REGT.

Nov 24

War Diary
10th L.N. Lancs
July 1917

112/37

Army Form C. 2118

WAR DIARY or INTELLIGENCE SUMMARY

10th Loyal North Lancs Regt

(Erase heading not required.)

Instructions regarding War Diaries and Intelligence Summaries are contained in F. S. Regs., Part II. and the Staff Manual respectively. Title Pages will be prepared in manuscript.

Place	Date	Hour	Summary of Events and Information	Remarks and references to Appendices
Kemmel	1/7/17		In bivouacs & shelters. Dr. Macnamara visits the Battalion. We move at nearer WYTSCHAETE. We have a lot of shrapnel over us at night	
nearer Kemmel	2/7/17		2Lt Lancaster joins the Battalion. We employ working parties for the 1st Australian Tunnelling Company working on the WOLVERGHEM—WYTSCHAETE ROAD.	
do	3/7/17		Carry on with working parties. Heavily shelled during the night with shrapnel. Two killed and 7 wounded.	
do	4/7/17		His Majesty the King visits the Corps area, and travels during hours.	
do	5/7/17		Still working w/ on the roads and at salvage.	
do	6/7/17		No change – nothing of particular interest.	
do	7/7/17		Working parties	
do	8/7/17		do	
do	9/7/17		do	

WAR DIARY
or
INTELLIGENCE SUMMARY

(Erase heading not required.)

Army Form C. 2118

Place	Date	Hour	Summary of Events and Information	Remarks and references to Appendices
Leau Kennel	9/7/17		Working parties. Sec. Lieut A.C. Baker rejoins the Battalion from England.	
do	10/7/17		Working parties in the camp and improving accomodation.	
do	11/7/17		do do	
do	12/7/17		Training as laid down during day, working parties under R.E. at night making Brigade N.B.	
do	13/7/17		Same as yesterday — no casualties	
do	14 —		Working parties at night 2/Lt R.E. Queenel wounded, 4 men killed & 11 wounded	
do	15 —		do	
do	16 —		do	
do	17 —		do	
do	18 —		Orders received for Brigade relief. Working parties during the night.	
On the Marsh	19 —		We relieve 1/8 Middlesex in front left sector of line. Bn. G. buys in front A.D. in support. Bn. H.Q. at TORREKEN Farm. relief complete by 1.30 a.m.	
do	20 —		Brigadier round in the morning. Intense bombardment all along from Govalos by ANZACS. We receive instructions regarding raid.	
do	21		Quiet day big working parties deepening Manchester Trench	

WAR DIARY or INTELLIGENCE SUMMARY

Army Form C. 2118

Place	Date	Hour	Summary of Events and Information	Remarks and references to Appendices
In the Trenches	22/7/17		Quiet day. One British aeroplane came down in No Mans Land. Pilots are very gallantly rescued by 2/Lt H N King and Sgt Dugdale	
do	23/7/17		"D" Coy carried out a raid this morning on RIFLE FARM. The Raiding party consisted of :- 2 Fighting Platoons, 2 extra Lewis gun teams, and an extra section to take charge of prisoners etc. All belonging to "D" Coy and commanded by Capt J.A GRAVET (M.C.) The object of this patrol was to enter RIFLE FARM, clear up situation and to take Prisoners. Having already lined up before dawn, in shell holes approx (N of N of Front Patrons) to O.23.a.4.5.0 they advanced on their objective O.23.c.4.5.8 at 4 a.m. (ZERO HOUR) Owing to Barrage on left being too much West and North, it necessitated a half right form. On arrival at eBay Farm it was found to be empty, but	

Army Form C. 2118

WAR DIARY
or
INTELLIGENCE SUMMARY
(Erase heading not required.)

Instructions regarding War Diaries and Intelligence Summaries are contained in F. S. Regs., Part II. and the Staff Manual respectively. Title Pages will be prepared in manuscript.

Place	Date	Hour	Summary of Events and Information	Remarks and references to Appendices
			Owing to fresh cigarette ends and matches it was obviously being used by night. From here to Rifle Farm Enclosure the Raiders were subjected to moderate Machine Gun and Rifle Fire. (When I say moderate, I do not mean slight.) On reaching the Enclosure the Raiders were met by very heavy Machine Gun and Rifle Fire. Machine guns appeared to be in position about O.23.b.34. and O.23.d.0.7. (two guns in the former and one in the latter.) Another Machine Gun was suspected in BEEK FARM. A trench running parallel to and close under Western edge of Enclosure was held by Boche; there were dislodged but continued to fire from centre of Enclosure. Our bombers got into the trench and proceeded in both directions. At 7.30 a.m. reinforcements of about 40 men came from direction of BEEK FARM over dead ground to entour 40 where they opened heavy rifle fire. The enemy by this time had obtained superiority of fire. Number of enemy at this moment was calculated to be at least equal to a	

1875 Wt. W593/826 1,000,000 4/15 J.B.C. & A.   A.D.S.S./Forms/C. 2118.

Army Form C. 2118

WAR DIARY
or
INTELLIGENCE SUMMARY
(Erase heading not required.)

Place	Date	Hour	Summary of Events and Information	Remarks and references to Appendices
			company rendering it impossible for us to actually get to the dug-outs. When these dug-outs, rifle grenade fire, was brought to bear. Two prisoners were taken near Western edge and close to Rifle Farm and some shelters destroyed but no identifications were found in the shelters. The allotted time being up, the signal to return was given at 7.27, by whistle. As soon as all our wounded had been got in (7.45am) the pre-arranged signal was given for barrages to slacken. Our telephone lines having been cut, communication was maintained by pigeons and runner. The following observations were made:— Rifle Farm is strongly held with outposts to Worth — and South flanks, by day, and advanced posts to the West by night. Smoke Barrage. The Machine Gun Barrage did not appear to be very heavy, but this might be because there was so much noise	

WAR DIARY
or
INTELLIGENCE SUMMARY
(Erase heading not required.)

Army Form C. 2118

Place	Date	Hour	Summary of Events and Information	Remarks and references to Appendices
			Concrete Dug-outs are on the left and centre of the enclosure the farm itself on the South Eastern corner of the enclosure is in ruins. Until about 4-30 a.m. the enemy's Barrage was most inaccurate, appearing first to the North and then to the South of the Farm. At this hour they placed it upon our shell-hole line. All our casualties were caused by rifle and Machine Gun fire and no instances of wounds caused by shell fire were found. O.C. Raiding Party, O.C. Parties and all members of the raid are convinced that the enemy suffered very heavy casualties and without any exaggeration is estimated at twice as heavy as ours, as more than ten men were seen to fall and if killed, without them twice this number appeared to be hit. This estimate is purely from our Rifle and M.G. Fire. Casualties from Shell Fire are unknown, but must have been considerable. It is known for certain that one en01 of the enemy Machine Gun Team was killed. The Officer who appeared to be in command of Rifle Farm	

WAR DIARY
or
INTELLIGENCE SUMMARY

Army Form C. 2118

Instructions regarding War Diaries and Intelligence Summaries are contained in F.S. Regs., Part II. and the Staff Manual respectively. Title Pages will be prepared in manuscript.

(Erase heading not required.)

Place	Date	Hour	Summary of Events and Information	Remarks and references to Appendices
Julla Kendles	24/1/17		seemed to have led a charmed life, his leadership and disregard of personal danger was admirable. Our total casualties were 8 killed 21 wounded	
do	25/1/17		Every one stands too to fire at aeroplane. Unfortunately it is our own luckily no damage was done. A quiet day — nothing to report.	
Beaver Hall	26/1/17		During the night of 25/26 we are relieved by the 4th Middlesex and retire to Beaver Hall (just behind Kemmel). Here we remain until 1 pm when we again move to DRANOUTRE.	
DRANOUTRE	27/1/17		Working parties found by all Coys.	
do	28/1/17		do	
do	29/1/17		Working parties and Church parade	
do	30/1/17		Working parties — nothing to report.	
do	31/1/17		"Z" Day. 63rd Brigade are under orders of 4st Div. We send a working party out to Rifle Farm. No casualties.	

10th (S) Bn. THE ......

Ja 25 Mr Gurney
10th L.N Lancers
Aug 1917

112/37.

WAR DIARY or INTELLIGENCE SUMMARY

10th Royal North Lancs Regt.

Place	Date	Hour	Summary of Events and Information	Remarks, and references to Appendices
DRANOUTRE	1/8/17		In Reserve huts. Find working parties every night.	
do	2/8/17		Move up as Brigade in Support to North Lancashire Village relieving the 5th Somersets	
ottawa	3/8/17		The weather still very rough - the men are soaked in their small shelters.	
Village				
do	4/8/17		Still finding working parties.	
do	5/8/17		The following honours & awards come through in Corps Routine Orders:-
2/Lt. H.N. King the Military Cross
21629 Sgt. G. Dugdale & 18861 Pte F. Heyes the D.C.M. awarded for enterprise gallantly East of Oostaverne on 22/7/17, for fetching in a wounded airman from No Mans Island under heavy fire.
Bar to M.C. to Capt. J.A. Gravett for daring reconnaissance, good leadership, and indomitable courage when in charge of raiding party east of Oostaverne.
2/Lt. H. Granth the Military Cross for gallant leadership - excellent escape to his men East of Oostaverne on 22/8/17.	

WAR DIARY
or
INTELLIGENCE SUMMARY

Army Form C. 2118

(Erase heading not required.)

Place	Date	Hour	Summary of Events and Information	Remarks and references to Appendices
Cunt			The Military medal to 13402 Pte T. Hall, 25748 Pte H. Hall, G. Clay, 15091 Cpl. F. Dymock, 12784 Sgt A. Dawson for gallantry + devotion to duty during the Raid on July 2nd. Bar to M.M. for 19505 L/C J.E. Wilcox + Cpl V.G. Burns for gallantry + skilful reconnaissance work during the Raid E of Oostaverne on 23 July 1917.	
North Lunes Village	6/8/17		Move from North Lunes Village to other side of Kemmel. The camp allotted to us is too insanitary to be occupied. We shift the camp to a more healthy spot and canyon.	
Near Kemmel	7/8/17		Move up as battalion in support with Batt. N.Q. Onraet wood and relieve the 9th Royal Welsh Fusiliers of the 19th Division. One Company in Van Hove line, one in Mauve line two in Ridge Defences.	
In the trenches	8/8/17		Improve condition of trenches	

WAR DIARY or INTELLIGENCE SUMMARY

Army Form C. 2118

(Erase heading not required.)

Place	Date	Hour	Summary of Events and Information	Remarks and references to Appendices
In the Trenches	9/8/17		In support. Do work for front Battalion – 2 casualties.	
do	10/8/17		ditto	
do	11/8/17		Our general Brig. Gen. R. C. Maclachlan is sniped in the early morning and killed. His death is deeply regretted. We lose a fine soldier and a great friend. During the night we relieve the 1st Royal Warwicks Regt in the line.	
do	12/8/17		A most unpleasant place. Far too much sniping going. Ours get to work. We claim two hits.	
do	13/8/17		Patrol of A. Coy goes out and obtains useful information. We are heavily shelled during the night.	
do	14/8/17		A good amount of salvage is done some 60 rifles are sent down. We take a new trench to the front line.	
do	15/8/17		The Battalion is relieved in the front line by the 8th Somersets	

WAR DIARY
or
INTELLIGENCE SUMMARY
(Erase heading not required.)

Army Form C. 2118

Place	Date	Hour	Summary of Events and Information	Remarks and references to Appendices
Camp	16/8/17		Off the 63rd Brigade. Everything very much quieter to-day. 2/Lt Breakell is hit in both legs by M.G. bullets. We return to IRISH House near Reninel. The men are very weary - it has been a great strain.	
near Reninel	17/8/17		General cleaning up and a real -sorely needed. Our new Brigadier — General IRVINE. DSO. visits the Battalion	
do	18/8/17		Working parties again. Coys working with Coy Commanders.	
do	19/8/17		Church Parade will 9th East Lancs Regt — a day of rest for some. Working parties. We receive warning order to relieve 63rd Brigade in the line the night of 21/22 nd.	
do	20/8/17		Battalion concert in the field. The Commanding Officer presents members of the Raiding Party who had won distinction with their ribbons.	
do	21/8/17			

WAR DIARY
or
INTELLIGENCE SUMMARY
(Erase heading not required.)

Army Form C. 2118

Place	Date	Hour	Summary of Events and Information	Remarks and references to Appendices
In the Trenches by Wytschaete	22/8/17		cont/ in ONRAET WOOD. Much quieter than before. We carry on with working parties & improving Batt. & Coy H.Q. and dugouts generally.	
do	23/8/17		Nothing special to report.	
do	24/8/17		We move up to relieve the 11th Royal Warwicks Regt as Right Front Battalion – relief completed without a casualty.	
Near Oostaverne	25/8/17		The line is much quieter than before. We encounter our enemies on wiring. Patrol is sent out and gets in touch with the enemy.	
do	26/8/17		The rain has set in and the whole place is one big mudheap. The men are again in a terrible condition. A practice S.O.S. is sent up consisting of 3 green Very Lights – Barrage opens in 80 seconds.	

WAR DIARY
INTELLIGENCE SUMMARY

Army Form C. 2118

Place	Date	Hour	Summary of Events and Information	Remarks and references to Appendices
... WYTCHAETE	27/8/17	22:30	We send out strong patrol with intent to snaffle a Boche in concrete shelter found to be occupied on previous night. Unfortunately it is not now occupied. One of the enemy is shot but party return empty handed.	
		2:30 am	Raid is carried out by 11th Royal Warwicks on Bee Farm. This is a post opposite our right Coy front. The prisoners are captured and the casualties very slight. Information is received from prisoners that a party of 100 "Sturmtruppen" were coming into position at 11am to raid our own front at Bee Farm. Though our raid this is frustrated.	
		4 pm	We are relieved in the line by the 10th Royal Fusiliers of the 111th Bde.	
Irish House	28/8/17		Every effort is made to get the men dry and clean again. After inspection etc. & rest.	
do	29/8/17		Kit inspections & Baths. Conference of Officers.	
do	30/8/17		11th Bde in the line.	
do	31/8/17		Received orders to relieve 116th Regt 39th Div. Received orders to relieve 116th Regt 39th Div.	

Lt Col Comdg

Va 26 112/37

War Diary
10th L. N. Lanc

Sept 1917

Army Form C. 2118

WAR DIARY
or
INTELLIGENCE SUMMARY 10th Royal North LANCS
(Erase heading not required.)

Instructions regarding War Diaries and Intelligence Summaries are contained in F. S. Regs., Part II. and the Staff Manual respectively. Title Pages will be prepared in manuscript.

Place	Date	Hour	Summary of Events and Information	Remarks and references to Appendices
1/9/17 IRISH HOUSE	1/9/17		Working parties and training inspections & fitting out tactical scheme	
	2/9/17		Battalion moves up to take over from the 13th Royal Sussex Regt in Brigade support in front of Voormezeele. We relieve without a casualty	
In the Trenches	3/9/17		Supply working parties for R.E. & Tunnellers near Hill 60. We send up a Ration O.C. party to lower the exchange of hats made by the 6th Bedfords. They have to advance therefore 150 yds.	
do	4/9/17		Working parties as usual. One casualty. A number of gas shells fall round our H.Q - no damage.	
do	5/9/17		Nothing special to report, thin shelling on huts & trenches observed and all possible improvements are being carried out.	
do	6/9/17		Working parties. We have two Naval Officers and 10 ratings attached to us for the night. They are extremely interested in everything.	

1875 Wt. W593/826 1,000,000 4/15 J.B.C. & A. A.D.S.S./Forms/C. 2118.

Army Form C. 2118

WAR DIARY
or
INTELLIGENCE SUMMARY
(Erase heading not required.)

Instructions regarding War Diaries and Intelligence Summaries are contained in F.S. Regs., Part II. and the Staff Manual respectively. Title Pages will be prepared in manuscript.

Place	Date	Hour	Summary of Events and Information	Remarks and references to Appendices
In the Trenches	7/9/17		Fairly quiet. We relieve the 10th Bedfords Regt in the line - Left sub-sector	
do	8/9/17		Posts are relied from Batt. H.Q. Everything is in perfect order. — a quiet night.	
do	9/9/17		Artillery more active to day. The 8th Bn. Royal Sussex carry out a raid on our immediate left. It is very altogether successful. We have large numbers of 19th Division up to reconnoitre the line. They are to relieve us in no understand. To-night the 6th Bedfords Regt carried out a raid on dugouts near JARROCKS FARM. It is not successful.	
do	10/9/17		Quiet all day showing thro' wound the line and O.P.'s. Shelling is considerably heavier to day. 2/Lt N L CARLINE joins the Battalion for duty. We are relieved by the 8th N. Staffs Regt and 10th Worcester Regt. of the 19th Division	
do	12/9/17	1am	Heavy shelling with mustard gas and shrapnel and H.E. We have to Rest. Our return our forward line. Impossible to get	

WAR DIARY
or
INTELLIGENCE SUMMARY

(Erase heading not required.)

Army Form C. 2118

Instructions regarding War Diaries and Intelligence Summaries are contained in F.S. Regs., Part II. and the Staff Manual respectively. Title Pages will be prepared in manuscript.

Place	Date	Hour	Summary of Events and Information	Remarks and references to Appendices
In the Trenches	13/9/17		through the barrage. 2/Lt. 6/L. Kelly is wounded. Also 2/Lt. C. Gill. We eventually arrive at Kettets near Vierstraat for the rest of the night.	
do	14/9/17	2pm.	Move on to Corunna Camp at Mont No17.a&a. Here we are in tents and pleasantly situated.	
Corunna Camp	15/9/17		Cleaning up and settling down into new camp. Bathing Inspections etc.	
do	16/9/17		Working parties again. When are we to leave them alone?	
do	17/9/17		Working parties. A few attend Church Parade held near our lines.	
do	18/9/17		Training, working parties etc.	
do	19/9/17		Inspection of Battalion by G.O.C. 112th Inf. Bde. Brig-General A.E. IRVINE D.S.O. Move up as Corps reserve from Mont Rouge at 6.30pm. to IRISH HOUSE.	

WAR DIARY or INTELLIGENCE SUMMARY

Army Form C. 2118

Place	Date	Hour	Summary of Events and Information	Remarks and references to Appendices
Corb/	19/9		In Battle Order. The Divisional General inspects the Battalion on the march.	
IRISH HOUSE	20/9		All fighting kit issued. Ready to move up at a few moments notice.	
		4.30pm	Receive orders to move to BOIS CARRÉ and relieve the 9th Royal No Lancs Regt.	
BOIS CARRÉ	21/9		Still waiting. We are to be the first to move.	
		4pm	Receive orders to move to IRISH HOUSE. This is cancelled and we are to go to Mon't Rouge. Behalf forthwith and arrive at 9.30pm.	
Corunna Camp	22/9	9am	Staff training.	
		10am	Warning Order to move up to the line.	
		5.30pm	Orders and move up to relieve 1st Camb, 118th Bde. 39th Division. 2Lt. H.N. KING and 2Lt. G. BRYDON are wounded also 20 men.	
In the line	23/9		Heavily shelled all day. We are just on the right of Tower Hamlets in Shrewsbury Forest. In support to 6th Bedfords Regt.	
	24/9		Move up to relieve the 6th Bedfords Regt in the line.	
	25/9		Still very rough—casualties mounting up.	
	26/9		All shelled — "the hottest" day of all.	

WAR DIARY or INTELLIGENCE SUMMARY

Army Form C. 2118

Instructions regarding War Diaries and Intelligence Summaries are contained in F.S. Regs., Part II. and the Staff Manual respectively. Title Pages will be prepared in manuscript.

(Erase heading not required.)

Place	Date	Hour	Summary of Events and Information	Remarks and references to Appendices
In the line	24/9		We are to be relieved today by the 10th Warwicks Regt & the 19th Division. They arrive and a very good relief is carried out. It is much quieter today. We move back near Dilmmel for the night and receive orders to move up as Brigade in Reserve. Our casualties are heavy being 9 Killed and wounded.	
Near Dilmmel	25/9/17		Move up to VIERSTRAAT under canvas and have to make ready a rest camp.	
Near Vierstraat	26/9/17		General cleaning up and inspections. Enemy aeroplanes bomb our Transport lines and kill two horses wounding 1.	
"	30/9		Church Parade.	

Signature
LT. COLONEL. COMDG.
10th (S) Bn. THE LOYAL NORTH LANCASHIRE REGT.

12/37

Vol 27

War Diary

of

10th (Service) Battalion Loyal North Lancashire Regiment

From 1st October 1917   To 31st October 1917

VOLUME 26

WAR DIARY
INTELLIGENCE SUMMARY

10th Local North'n R.S. Regt

Army Form C. 2118

Place	Date	Hour	Summary of Events and Information	Remarks and references to Appendices
Willibeek Camp	1/10/17		The following Officers joined the Battalion yesterday from England. 2/Lt F. CATTERALL, CRANE H., BUCHAN J., DILLON H. We are to stay here until we relieve the 63rd + 111th Bde. 2/Lt J.A. JACKSON, and CADBECK C.H.	
do	2/10/17		Commanding Officers parade in full marching Order for inspection	
do	3/10/17		ditto Inspection of iron rations etc.	
do	4/10/17		We are waiting to move up to the BASSEVILLEBEEK Sector. The 8th E.Lancs Regt have gone up in Reserve to LARCHWOOD Tunnels to support 63rd and 111th Bdes when going over.	
do	5/10/17		We hear that the Bedfords are to go up next — in fact have gone. We next so called receive orders to relieve the 13th KRRC. in the line. We meet so called guides at MOUNT SORREL. A terrible journey — the worst we have ever had. A long weary tiresome haul across desolate swampy ground. Caught in live barrages. Eventually arrive at our destination just in front of Tower Hamlets. Our casualties are heavy going in.	
Tower Hamlets			It is Quelia this morning. The reports from the Coys show the line to be still in the way in places. However this is soon put ...	

WAR DIARY or INTELLIGENCE SUMMARY

Army Form C. 2118

Place	Date	Hour	Summary of Events and Information	Remarks and references to Appendices
Tercen Hamlets	7/10		straight. There are rumours of an expected enemy attack. Nothing however comes of it. Unfortunately our rations do not reach us to-night. The ration party get badly shelled and the travelling is extremely difficult even if one could find the way. We send out a Patrol to Lewis House - most certainly it is occupied.	
do	8/10		A lively day started by a practice barrage. Patrol goes out to Juke Coy's and finds it occupied very strongly. Heavy shelling all day - a lovely barrage on Besseville beek, KeuIH. Simpson is wounded. More trouble with the Rations. Still another practice barrage.	
do	9/10		Zero hour is 5.20am. We have to capture our task. 2/Lt A.C. BAKER, Sgt BALL and Queen of C. Coy, Sgt DUFFY and Queen of A. Coy go off to do the task. They are shot from the outset with annihilating M.G. fire and Coy get more than a few yds. 2/Lt A.C. is badly wounded. Nothing but stays on. Unfortunately it is not a success	J.B.C.

Army Form C. 2118

WAR DIARY
or
INTELLIGENCE SUMMARY
(Erase heading not required.)

Place	Date	Hour	Summary of Events and Information	Remarks and references to Appendices
Tower Hamlets	10/10		put a very gallant attack has been made. The names of 2/Lt. A.C. BAKER and Sgt. G. BALL are especially worthy of note. The names of Lieuts P.Bee, W.J.Plant and H.CRANK appear in the Gazette as Captains. 2/Lt. F. HAYES as Lieut. We are to be relieved to night by the 8th Lincolns Regt. A fairly quiet day. The night is very rough and the shelling is heavy. Extreme difficulty is found in getting the relieving battalion in. Relief is complete by daylight and we make tracks for Willebeek Cant again.	
Willebeek Camp	11/10		We arrive here during the morning very tired and absolutely worn out. The men are also quite cheerful though rather badly shaken. It has been a terrible time.	

WAR DIARY
or
INTELLIGENCE SUMMARY

Army Form C. 2118

Place	Date	Hour	Summary of Events and Information	Remarks and references to Appendices
Millebeek Camp	12/10		We understand the Division is to be relieved at last – We have heard this before however! The day is spent in cleaning up. Our casualties we find are 65 o. Ranks 2 Officers killed and wounded.	
Corunna Camp.	13/10		We receive orders to move to Corunna Camp. We joyfully prepare to move. Things are looking brighter!	
do	14/10		General cleaning up and inspection. We have not had much time so far. It is Sunday. There is Church Parade for some of us.	
do	15/10		We receive orders to make a composite battalion with the 5th E. Lancs Reg¹ under command of Lt Col Hennessy N.Z. Staff. to work in rear of YPRES on the roads under the 2nd ANZAC Corps. The rest is apparently another rumour. We are carried up in buses nearly into YPRES then march to the camp. Every thing is very vague, and we can't damn well	

WAR DIARY
or
INTELLIGENCE SUMMARY

Army Form C. 2118

Place	Date	Hour	Summary of Events and Information	Remarks and references to Appendices
YPRES	16/10		We "turn to" in our accustomed way and soon things look more cheerful. We hope to have more room tomorrow.	
do	17/10		We send working parties to work on the St Jean — Wieltje Road under the Road Construction Coys. We are shelled periodically and also bombed continually. We are seems to worry very much about it.	
do	18/10		The same as yesterday. Working parties. It is cold and miserable. Major C.G. De PREE joins the Battalion as Second in Command.	
do	19/10		Nil.	
do	20/10		Fairly quiet to-day. Working parties as usual. Heavily bombed all 6 p.m. Shelled throughout the night. We have killed and wounded — Working parties.	

Army Form C. 2118

WAR DIARY
or
INTELLIGENCE SUMMARY
(Erase heading not required.)

Instructions regarding War Diaries and Intelligence Summaries are contained in F. S. Regs., Part II. and the Staff Manual respectively. Title Pages will be prepared in manuscript.

Place	Date	Hour	Summary of Events and Information	Remarks and references to Appendices
YPRES	21/10		Working parties and usual training.	
do	22/10		Working in the morning and have orders to return to MONT NOIR area. We are to go to CORUNNA CAMP. We are relieved by 111th Bde.	
		2pm	Buses and return to Camp. Here we find a draft of 135 O.Ranks Mostly A.3. men.	
Corunna Camp	23/10		General cleaning up and inspection of draft. 2Lts. Irons, Law and Peachy join the Battalion.	
do	24/10		Battalion and Company training begins.	
do	25/10		Training continues. The undermentioned men are awarded the Military Medal. No.36940 Pte R.Hurst 17604 Pte GREENWOOD. R. No 36973 Pte T. GREENHALGH 7017618 Pte R.Hardman No 14162 Pte G. HARTLEY for continuous bravery and devotion to duty East of YPRES from 1st to 10th October.	

WAR DIARY or INTELLIGENCE SUMMARY

Army Form C. 2118

(Erase heading not required.)

Place	Date	Hour	Summary of Events and Information	Remarks and references to Appendices
Louvrin Camp	26/10		Battalion moves to LOCRE Area and is billeted in BIRR Barracks. Dry and comfortable billets.	
Birr Barracks	27/10			
LOCRE	28/10		Route March and Battalion Training	
do	29/10		Church Parade Service	
do	30/10		Battalion training. – Physical Drill Bayonet fighting Gas Rest. Drill. Saluting, Lewis & Rouline lecture. Stretcher bearer training.	
do	30/10		Battalion training.	
do	31/10		Route march over Mont Noir – Mont Rouge, Dranoutre Locre. The undermentioned Officer and N.C.O. are awarded as under. 2/Lt A.C. BAKER. The Military Cross, 13894 Sergt W. Horridge and 33806 L/Sgt G. BALL the Distinguished Conduct Medal W gallantry, initiation and devotion to duty east of YPRES on October 8th 1917.	[signature]

Lucius Cama
LT. COLONEL, COMDG.
10th (S) Bn. THE LOYAL NORTH LANCASHIRE REGT.

WAR DIARY 10th Royal North Lancs Regt
or
INTELLIGENCE SUMMARY

WO 28

Place	Date	Hour	Summary of Events and Information	Remarks and references to Appendices
LOCRE	1/11/19		Training as laid down for trench warfare.	
do	2/11/17		Rehearsal for Commemoration Service. Naval Battalion training.	
do	3/11		Route march in morning and Brigade Bomb competition in which we are the winners.	
do	4/11		Sunday. Commemoration service for those who have fallen in the 112th Bde. The whole Brigade is on parade. The service ends with a march past the Divisional General.— General Bruce Williams C.B. D.S.O.	
do	5/11		Canyon with training as before.	
do	6/11		Recur orders that we are to move on the 8th inst and relieve the 19th Division in the Hollebeke — Hill 60 — Shrewsbury Forest sector.	
do	7/11		We are to be right sector to 11th Royal Warwick Regt.	
do	8/11		Move up to Bois Carre and relieve the 7th South Lancashire Regt.	J.W.W.

Army Form C. 2118

WAR DIARY
or
INTELLIGENCE SUMMARY
(Erase heading not required.)

Instructions regarding War Diaries and Intelligence Summaries are contained in F.S. Regs., Part II. and the Staff Manual respectively. Title Pages will be prepared in manuscript.

Place	Date	Hour	Summary of Events and Information	Remarks and references to Appendices
Bois Carré	9/11/17		Move up by companies to relieve the 10th Worcester Regt. in Spoil Bank Tunnels in Battalion in Reserve. An easy relief and no casualties.	
in the trenches or at Spoil Bank	10/11		Became aware that we are to move up on the night of 11/12th and extend the Brigade line to our right, near Hollebeke. Our dispositions will be as follows. 1 Company in the Front line, 1 Company in Close support, 1 Company at Bove Tunnels with Batt. H.Q., and 1 Company at Spoil Bank. Relieve one company of 2n Bedfords Regt. and two companies of 17th Kings Liverpools Regt. A good relief — no casualties.	
do.	11/11		A fairly quiet day. The line is overlooking all things very good. We are able to get our rations up to H.Q. and support easily by day.	
do	12/11		With a duck board trench to the support line.	
do	13/11		Still quiet. O.C. by (Lieut N. Booth) sends out patrol to definitely settle position of enemy post opposite our line.	J.W.B.M. 7/W/B/M

WAR DIARY
or
INTELLIGENCE SUMMARY
(Erase heading not required.)

Army Form C. 2118

Place	Date	Hour	Summary of Events and Information	Remarks and references to Appendices
In the Trenches	13/11		cont. Our ideas are corroborated by patrol.	
do	14/11	1 am.	2/Lt Bochan and Sgt Dugdale (D.C.M) go out as reconnoitring patrol. Two of the enemy are surprised and eventually driven into the hands of Cpl. Shenton of C Coy. who takes them prisoner. They appear to be men of the 3rd Reserve Prussian Guard, who were going out to their post when they were met by 2/Lt Bochan and the Sgt.	
		5 pm	One section of C Coy go out to occupy enemy post and if possible capture relief coming up. We carry out an inter company relief. All except front line coy are relieved by daylight.	
do	15/11		The enemy are more active today. During our air fight two British and one German aeroplanes are brought down. We discover and bury the remains of Lieut. Middleton R.F.C. who was brought down some few days ago.	

Army Form C. 2118

WAR DIARY
or
INTELLIGENCE SUMMARY
(Erase heading not required.)

Instructions regarding War Diaries and Intelligence Summaries are contained in F. S. Regs., Part II. and the Staff Manual respectively. Title Pages will be prepared in manuscript.

Place	Date	Hour	Summary of Events and Information	Remarks and references to Appendices
In the Trenches	16/11		A quiet day. Two patrols go out from "D" Coy and good information obtained.	
do	17/11		The quietest day of all, we are relieved by the 10th Royal Fusiliers Regt. Three coys relieved by daylight. and the Battalion returns to BOIS CARRE	
BOIS Carre	18/11		General cleaning up and working parties.	
do	19/11		Every one out on working parties	
do	20/11		ditto	
do	21/11		ditto	
do	22/11		ditto	
do	23/11		ditto	
do	24/11		ditto	
do	25/11		The Brigade goes into Divisional Reserve in the LA CLYTTE area.	

WAR DIARY
or
INTELLIGENCE SUMMARY

Army Form C. 2118

Place	Date	Hour	Summary of Events and Information	Remarks and references to Appendices
LACUTTE	25/11	Con	The Battalion moves to MURRUMBIDGEE CAMP. — a hutted and fairly dry camp with poor accommodation.	
do	26/11		Bathing & cleaning generally, inspection of kit etc. The following officers joined the Battalion to day. 2/Lts E WRIGLEY and J. F. Mills. and are posted to B and A. Coys respectively.	
do	27/11		Improvements to camp. Musketry class started. Individual training.	
do	28/11		Divisional Salvage scheme in in which the whole of the 112d Bde takes part. A large area is cleared of Camps kits etc.	
do	29/11		Salvage operations carried on as yesterday.	
do	30/11		Training and recreation. Football etc. Nothing of special interest to report.	

Susan Ermer
LT. COLONEL, COMDG..
10th (S) Bn. THE LOYAL NORTH LANCASHIRE REGT.

WAR DIARY or **INTELLIGENCE SUMMARY**

Army Form C. 2118

(Erase heading not required.)

Place	Date	Hour	Summary of Events and Information	Remarks and references to Appendices
ACIyHe	1/12/17		Training at Morrombidgee Camp	
do	2/12		Church Parade for all denominations.	
do	3/12		Training and revetting of huts. Construction of sandmodel. Laying track through camp	
do	4/12		Preparations for going into the line tomorrow. Whale oiling feet etc.	
do	5/12	1.15pm	Move up on Light Railway to Skoll Bank to relieve 1/6 Att Middlesex Reg'. in Left centre sub-section – Belgian Wood and Jarrocks Farm sector. "A" Coy Aufhoff and Tourpelle by 8pm. "A" Coy on the right front "B" Coy left front, "C" Coy aufhoff and "D" Coy at Hill 60 in Reserve.	
do	6/12	4am	A fairly quiet day. Both companies acid-out a patrol under an officers. Good information obtained.	
do	7/12		Enemy artillery rather more active to day. A patrol out from each Coy again. Kept in touch with our flanks. Our right company is very suddenly properly using possible precaution is taken against trench fel. Socks hoorded many had a sent at thee times during the night. Wads	

WAR DIARY or INTELLIGENCE SUMMARY

Army Form C. 2118

Place	Date	Hour	Summary of Events and Information	Remarks and references to Appendices
Kukiedi	8/12		It is unusual to-day but a thaw has set in and the ground is very muddy. The conditions of life in the front line will be much worse now. Patrols are again out from each coy.	
do	9/12	3.20 A.M.	The enemy raided our No 9 post and received a good reception. The post was approached by two parties on North & South flanks. A barrage was put down just behind the post and under cover of this the wire was cut and the raiders attacked. The Garrison of the post consisted of 25238 CpI J. Grundod, (in charge) 32897 Pte G.E. White, 31792 Pte Hutton J. 31954 Pte E. Compton and 20352 Pte J. Gregan. As soon as the bombs began to fall and the raiders were seen the garrison rushed from the post to meet them. Pte White alone engaged two of the enemy fighting a hand to hand conflict with the enemy though severely wounded by the butts of rifles and will no doubt then be fought on eventually killing one and taking the other (a Sergt Major) Prisoner. One cannot speak too highly of this man	

WAR DIARY or INTELLIGENCE SUMMARY

determination and gallantry. His action was undoubtedly the cause of the success. Cpl Gricrod displayed coolness and judgement working his Lewis Gun with deadly effect. He was most ably supported by the remainder of the garrison who succeeded in beating off the attack causing heavy casualties. The raiders were estimated to be between 20 and 25 strong. Of these three were killed and two were taken prisoners. (One died in the post after). Both Lally attacked Cpl Gricrod followed them up firing his Lewis Gun and caused several more casualties. It is hard to estimate the destruction done owing to the swampy and almost impassable nature of the ground. 2/Lt. C.F. CATTERALL was in command of this part of hole and displayed coolness, judgement and initiative showing a ready grasp of the situation and posting his men accordingly. The dispositions of his men during the attack was

Fauquissart	10/12	have been quiet with the same resolute spirit and suffered a serious loss. All our men with the exception of Pte White ~~are wounded~~ were unhurt.
do	11/12	The rest of the day passed quietly. The enemy artillery are more active today but generally it is quiet. We send out patrols as usual.
do	12/12	Quieter to-day but many balloons are up and gunners register on various targets. Nothing special to report. Generally quiet. Some shelling of Battalion H.Q.
do	13/12	We are relieved to day by 13th Kings Royal Rifle Corps. Quite successful but very late back night and had gone to bed in confusion.
Ridge Wood	14/12	Arrived at Ridge Wood in relief of 10th York & Lancs Regt.

WAR DIARY
or
INTELLIGENCE SUMMARY.
(Erase heading not required.)

Army Form C. 2118.

Place	Date	Hour	Summary of Events and Information	Remarks and references to Appendices
Ridge Wood	15/12		We start on working parties. Every man out including the Revel and as usual.	
"	16/12		Nothing special to report. Working parties	
"	17/12		Ditto	
"	18/12		Ditto	
"	19/12		Ditto	
"	20/12		Ditto	
"	21/12		Move to Reserve Area and take over from 8th Lincoln Regt. A heavy frost has set in and the conditions are very bad.	
"	22/12		Working parties still continue — The men are getting a rather bad time. There is a noticeable decline in the general physique of the battalion — it is inevitable	
"	23/12		Working parties — when are they to end? The men are rather worn out. Big long hours and constant strain. Preparations for Christmas are in hand.	

WAR DIARY
or
INTELLIGENCE SUMMARY.
(Erase heading not required.)

Army Form C. 2118.

Place	Date	Hour	Summary of Events and Information	Remarks and references to Appendices
24Dn	24/12		Working parties. Inspections etc. Real winter weather has set in now	
Murrombidgee	25/12		Christmas Day. As far as possible a day of rest. A big dinner for all members of the Battalion. We are very lucky to be out of the line to	
CAMP			enjoy it. Every thing a great success. Concert in the Recreation Hut in the evening	
"	26/12		Note very much enthusiasm for work this morning. A few working parties go out. The new foot treatment is continued.	
"	27/12		Training as far as possible. Special inspection of gas appliances. We know that a lot of gas is being used in the line now.	
"	28/12		Training and preparations for moving up into the line on the 29th.	
The Trenches	29/12		We receive orders to relieve 4th MIDDLESEX REGT in line at BELGIAN WOOD and JARROCKS FARM Sector. Complete relief by 7.30 p.m. Front line, "B" Coy left, "A" Coy right, "C" Coy Support, "D" Coy reserve	
	29/12		Quiet day. Nothing to report.	
	30/12		Quiet day. Good patrol by "A" Coy officer and two other ranks and useful information obtained. Four shells dropped just outside Bn. H.Q.	

WAR DIARY
or
INTELLIGENCE SUMMARY

(Erase heading not required.)

Army Form C. 2118

Place	Date	Hour	Summary of Events and Information	Remarks and references to Appendices
In the Trenches	1/11/18		Very quiet day. Between 7 and 9 p.m. 24 SERVICE and 2 o.r. did a very good patrol. Advanced to within 50 yards of enemy post and fired several rifle grenades. The result was excellent for very lights and machine guns were fired instantly giving the whole position and strength away. All the men are in excellent spirits as the huts are dry and fairly comfortable.	
	2/11/18		Quiet along the Battalion Front. Patrolling and wiring was carried on during the night.	
	3/11/18		Fair amount of shelling around Batt. H.Q. between 6 and 6.30 p.m. Wiring was continued during the night. The good weather is still holding out and the men are in good spirits.	
	4/11/18		Very quiet. Nothing to report.	
	5/11/18		Quiet all day. We are relieved in the evening by the 13th K.R.R.C. Relief complete by 7.45 p.m. Battalion moves by light railway from SPOIL BANK to RIDGE WOOD CAMP in Bois S'upont.	

WAR DIARY
or
INTELLIGENCE SUMMARY

Army Form C. 2118

Place	Date	Hour	Summary of Events and Information	Remarks and references to Appendices
Ridge Wood	6/1/18		The day is spent in general cleaning up. Our C.O. Lt.Col. S.A. Cameron is awarded the D.S.O. and accepts the hearties Congratulations of the Battalion. Working parties all day.	
"	7/1/18		ditto	
"	8/1/18		Transport moves in Advance by Road to WALLON CAPPEL. The day is spent in preparing for the road.	
"	9/1/18		Entrain at DICKEBUSCH station at 2.30 pm & detrain at EBBLINGHAM at 4.50 pm. March to billets at WALLON CAPPEL arriving there at 9.15 pm. Very comfortable billets but scattered.	
WALLON CAPPEL	11/1/18		The day is spent in cleaning up generally.	
"	12/1/18		Coys start training in Musketry, close order drill, Gas drill & P.T. working from 8.30 am to 12.30 pm. Afternoons to recreational training in the form of football	

WAR DIARY
or
INTELLIGENCE SUMMARY

Army Form C. 2118

Place	Date	Hour	Summary of Events and Information	Remarks and references to Appendices
WALLON CAPPEL	13/1/18		Church parade on "A" Coys parade ground at 12 noon. Afternoon spent in football. Reg.t V. Learn. V. Canadian Reserve Park. Result 4–2 in favour of Canadians	
"	14/1/18		The weather is sadly changed and snow has set in but training is carried on as usual.	
"	15/1/18		Training including route marching Musketry, firing, physical training.	
"	16/1/18		The weather is very bad to day training in the open is almost impossible	
"	17/1/18		Preparing for the G.O.C. inspection on Saturday. It is too wet for the men to be out. The Divisional Commander inspects some of the billets.	
"	18/1/18		Another wet day – nothing special to report.	
"	19/1/18		Commander of the whole battalion and	

WAR DIARY
or
INTELLIGENCE SUMMARY.
(Erase heading not required.)

Army Form C. 2118.

Place	Date	Hour	Summary of Events and Information	Remarks and references to Appendices
WALLON CAPPEL	19/1/18 20/1/18		and Rexepoort. We are to move to the ground area for work under the C.R.E on the Corps "A" line. The whole of the 112th Brigade moves up. Lieu T. Moore M.C.	
"	21/1/18		Entrain at EBBLINGHAM at 9.30am and arrive at DICKE BUSCH at 12.30pm. Here we detrain and march off to SCOTTISH WOOD and Forrester Camp. Working parties commence. Two hundred and fifty men out daily, digging and wiring trenches, wiring reserve line and carrying material	
VIERSTRAAT	22/1/18		Working parties. The line is fairly quiet and we have no casualties. The men are quite comfortable, living in dry Nissen Bow Huts. The ground is very wet and waterlogged and badly needs draining	
"	23/1/18		Working parties as usual and work round the camps as far as is possible with available men and material	
"	24/1/18		Working parties ditto	
"	25/1/18 26/1/18		nothing special to report	

WAR DIARY
or
INTELLIGENCE SUMMARY.
(Erase heading not required.)

Army Form C. 2118.

Place	Date	Hour	Summary of Events and Information	Remarks and references to Appendices
Vierstraat	27/1/18		No working parties to day Voluntary Church parade & all denominations. Our dead knell has rung! The news has been received to day that we are to be disbanded. For the moment no one can realise it. The Battalion that has been our home for so long, that we have fought and worked for is to be broken up. The Battalion which we have all prided ourselves in being a member of and whose good name has been unsullied since the outbreak of hostilities is to fade away and be a thing of the past. It is indeed hard! Both Officers and men in spite of this blow have decided to carry out the task of this ability the splendid traditions of the Battalion to the last.	
"	28/1/18		Working parties as usual - nothing of interest to report.	
"	29/1/18		ditto	
"	30/1/18		Receive orders that we are to move back on the 1st February to CAMPAGNE near ST. OMER.	
"	31/1/18		Working parties as before - nothing of interest	

EO Emoux Lt Col

WAR DIARY or INTELLIGENCE SUMMARY

Army Form C. 2118.

Place	Date	Hour	Summary of Events and Information	Remarks and references to Appendices
Westvraak	1/2/16		Carry on with working parties	
	2/2/16		Working parties as good and have to return. No arrivals casualties	
	3/2/16		Working tactics. We are to move to RACQUINGHEM tomorrow	
	4/2/16		Boots. We are relieved by the 13th Bn Rifle Brigade & the 11th Rifle Brigade. Train parade camp at 11noon & train at DICKEBUSCH at 1.15 p.m. Have a good run down to EBBLINGHEM where we detrain and march to RACQUINGHEM where we arrive about 6pm. The Billets though scattered are dry and comfortable	
Racquinghem	5/2/16		Cleaning up for the Commanding Officers inspection	
do	6/2/16		The C.O. inspects the Battalion in full marching Order - a good turnout. The Battalion starts training in Musketry, Bayonet, Field Routemarch etc. according to programme of training	
do	7/2/16			
	8/2/16		Training as per programme. Recreational training in the afternoon. There is a big improvement in the men now they are getting footspell and a healthy life	

T2134. Wt. W708—776. 500000. 4/15. Sir J. C. & S.

WAR DIARY or INTELLIGENCE SUMMARY

Army Form C. 2118.

Place	Date	Hour	Summary of Events and Information	Remarks and references to Appendices
NGEING HEN	17/4 1/2/16		School Parade for all denominations.  We understand that we are to move up to the reinforcement camp and therefore expect it to be the last opportunity of having a Battalion parade, a parade is ordered for the purpose of trooping the Battalion flag which has fluttered over us for so long and through many trying periods. The ceremony is carried out as under:-	
		1	The Battalion formed up in hollow square, flag in centre, in inside the square and the Commanding Officer (Lt Col E.A. CAMERON D.S.O) reclaims the object of the parade.	
		2	The Battalion fix bayonets and present to the Flag while the Drums sound the General Salute	
		3	Flag taken in procession round ranks, preceded by the Band playing the Regimental March Past, followed by all the Officers, 2/Lt H.J. LANCASTER carried the flag.	
		4	The flag is furled and mounted. Revue Arms	
		5	The Commanding Officer delivers his farewell speech to the Battalion	

WAR DIARY or INTELLIGENCE SUMMARY

Army Form C. 2118

Place	Date	Hour	Summary of Events and Information	Remarks and references to Appendices
cont.			in a few well chosen words. The I men are deeply affected by the way they realise the splendid work that their Commanding Officer has done for them in the past and how the interests of the Battalion have always come foremost in his thoughts. The ceremony is ended by the Regt Sgt. Major BROMLEY marching the Battalion past the Officer.	
RACQUINGHEM.	12/2/18		Training as usual.	
"	13/2/18		ditto Orders are received to move to WIPPENHOEK on the 15th inst.	
"	14/2/18		Carry on with the training and prepare to move.	
"	15/2/18		Leave RACQUINGHEM at 8am and entrain at EBBINGHEM at 10.30am. Major General A. Bruce-Williams C.B. D.S.O. our Divisional Commander bids goodbye to the Officers and men of the Battalion. We detrain at ABEELE and march to WIPPENHOEK	

WAR DIARY or INTELLIGENCE SUMMARY

Army Form C. 2118

Place	Date	Hour	Summary of Events and Information	Remarks and references to Appendices
DICKEBUSCH	6/2/15		We came under the administration of the 22nd Corps of the 4th Army	
do	17/2/15		as Sirhind troops available as reinforcements. Everyone with leaving whilst awaiting instructions from G.H.Q. So far all the men are in huts and are comparatively comfortable	
do	18/2		Meeting of Officers interest to units.	
do	19/2		It is notified that the 1006th Bn. has pd North Lancashire Regt. becomes further on the 21st February.	
do	20/2		Men to be made up to 1100 strong and become No. 15 Entrenching Battalion and are awaiting orders to move to the 5th Army	
do	21/2		This day will be well remembered by every member of the Battalion as the day on which it lost North Lancs Regt.	

Place	Date	Hour	Summary of Events and Information	Remarks and references to Appendices
Nieuport	5.11.14	cont	The men realise what their Battalion means to them and it is a sad day for those who have fought hard and often to feel the good name of the Regiment imperilled. They look back with pride on the fighting record of the "10th" and fully appreciate the recognition of the Commander in Chief on his having mentioned the Battalion on more than one occasion in his despatches. In spite of the heavy blow that has fallen upon them both officers [and] men [have determined?] [Shaw?] and [illegible] have borne [?] the record [?] [determination?] to [illegible] the 10th (1st Bn) Royal North [Lancs?]	

www.ingramcontent.com/pod-product-compliance
Lightning Source LLC
Chambersburg PA
CBHW080913230426
43667CB00015B/2672